# COOKING
## ON THE ROAD

# COOKING
## ON THE ROAD
John Rakowski

ANDERSON
WORLD, INC.

Library of Congress Cataloging in Publication Data

Rakowski, John, 1922-
    Cooking on the road.

    Includes index.
    1. Outdoor cookery. I. Title.
TX823.R25            641.5'78            78-65977
ISBN 0-89037-200-4

*Cover photography by Wayne Glusker*

Anderson World, Inc.
Mountain View, California

To Pauline
who tasted and advised

# Contents

Preface . . . . . . . . . . . . . . . . . . . . . . . . . . . . . . . . . . . . ix

**Part One: Getting Organized**

The Logistics of the Bike-Kitchen . . . . . . . . . . . . . . . . . . . .3
Let's Go Shopping. . . . . . . . . . . . . . . . . . . . . . . . . . . . . .18
That Capricious One-Burner . . . . . . . . . . . . . . . . . . . . . . .24
Let's Get Organized. . . . . . . . . . . . . . . . . . . . . . . . . . . . .36
Down to Basics . . . . . . . . . . . . . . . . . . . . . . . . . . . . . . .42
Let's Practice. . . . . . . . . . . . . . . . . . . . . . . . . . . . . . . . .48
Cleaning Up the Mess . . . . . . . . . . . . . . . . . . . . . . . . . . .52
Cooking for One . . . . . . . . . . . . . . . . . . . . . . . . . . . . . . .57
Cheap or High on the Hog? . . . . . . . . . . . . . . . . . . . . . . . .61
Natural Foods by June Clifton . . . . . . . . . . . . . . . . . . . . . 69

**Part Two: Recipes**

Meats. . . . . . . . . . . . . . . . . . . . . . . . . . . . . . . . . . . . . .77
Chicken. . . . . . . . . . . . . . . . . . . . . . . . . . . . . . . . . . . .110
Seafood. . . . . . . . . . . . . . . . . . . . . . . . . . . . . . . . . . . .117
Bread and Eggs . . . . . . . . . . . . . . . . . . . . . . . . . . . . . . .124
Traveling Without Meat. . . . . . . . . . . . . . . . . . . . . . . . . .137
Desserts. . . . . . . . . . . . . . . . . . . . . . . . . . . . . . . . . . . .162
One-Person Recipes . . . . . . . . . . . . . . . . . . . . . . . . . . . .169

**Appendix**

Some Hints . . . . . . . . . . . . . . . . . . . . . . . . . . . . . . . . . 179
Staples for Cooking on the Road . . . . . . . . . . . . . . . . . . . 181
Foods for Hot Weather Riding . . . . . . . . . . . . . . . . . . . . . 182
High Altitude Cooking . . . . . . . . . . . . . . . . . . . . . . . . . . 184
Spices and Condiments . . . . . . . . . . . . . . . . . . . . . . . . . . 186

**Glossary** . . . . . . . . . . . . . . . . . . . . . . . . . . . . . . . . . 191

**Index** . . . . . . . . . . . . . . . . . . . . . . . . . . . . . . . . . . . 195

# Preface

If you can read you can cook. After all, what is cooking if not a series of repeatable formulas, applied with intelligence and care? You don't have to be initiated into its mysteries. An afternoon's reading of a few of the cookbooks found on any library's shelves, and some practice on a few guinea pigs, should suffice to make anyone capable, if not proficient, in that ancient, overrated art.

Or so I used to think. That was before I began cooking during bicycle tours. A new set of rules immediately applied to what I considered a simple discipline. Food seemed to stick more readily in the open air. The stove acted up, boiling when I said simmer. Each meal that I made required exactly one more pan than I had with me, and I regularly ran out of one of the needed ingredients.

Swarms of insects insisted that I share their company at the redwood table. Fellow bikers made pests of themselves too. They tasted, commented, and volunteered well-meaning but distracting aid—I couldn't very well tell them to go into the other room, unlike at home with my family.

What to do? Neither camping cookbooks, concentrating on trailers and recreational vehicles, nor wilderness cookbooks, written around the needs of a backpacker, were helpful. I couldn't carry a quarter ton of multiburner stove, oven, and refrigerated food like the RVs. Plans for a grub box were of no use to me.

I didn't want to depend on prepackaged, dehydrated food either, except for condiments and a few staples. Backpacking food was not only expensive and hard to find, but its taste wasn't consistently good. And its being light and compact didn't mean that much to me; I could always carry a few pounds in my bags for a couple of miles after shopping.

Nor did I have time for the elaborate preparation and the slow cooking that were often required by those cookbooks. They assumed long stays in campgrounds, with semipermanent setups and time enough to construct reflector ovens and a bed of coals for roasting. That wasn't my style, even if I had the time. I would rather travel for the extra hours than cook. Grocery stops were made just before arriving at the campsite, usually late in the day. I'd have little patience for elaborate rituals.

Mine was a peculiar problem; not addressed by the available camp cooking guides. The problem must be common to other bicyclists, I thought, as well as those who tour by motorcycle, moped, and scooter. In addition, the long-distance hitchhikers, in this country and overseas, who live out of the packs on their backs must also face the same dilemma. Even those in small cars have more in common with two-wheel travelers than with RV and trailer users.

This book is the result of considering those questions and matching them with my experiences on the road. I've written it to help meet the needs of that kind of travel, especially the stresses of a long tour. The book addresses that whole group of wanderers whose personal trip is touring rather than camping, the pilgrims who travel lightly and have little room in their packs for a lot of equipment.

They are unlike either backpackers or the RV crowd, since they are limited in what they can carry but able to shop in small quantities daily. They set up a temporary kitchen each night—in a campground, a rest stop, park, or on a tree stump — and break it down to move quickly on the next day.

It's obvious that a small guide such as this cannot teach a novice the art of cooking. I don't even think of myself as a cook. Rather, I'm a bicyclist who learned to cook on the road, more in self-defense than from love of that art—defense against bad cafe food, high costs, and the uncertainties of finding restaurants open.

My intention is simply to get the beginner started and to point out some of the pitfalls he or she can encounter. Those with cooking experience may also find the book useful for we can all learn from each other's discoveries and mistakes. And I include a number of recipes that are easy to use while traveling on the road, enough to last a few months without repeating any.

I've tried out all the meals, some of them dozens of times. There were none I disliked, but I appreciate that my tastes may differ from the reader's. No matter. The recipes can be changed by the addition, deletion, or substitution of ingredients, something you'll feel confident enough to do after cooking for a few weeks on tour.

Please don't misunderstand my concern with time and simplicity. I don't eat out of cans, and I don't buy convenience foods that are ready for the pot. My prejudice is that an idiot can make a better meal than one prepared in Minneapolis, at the kitchen factories of General Mills; not to mention that the latter is probably full of preservatives, artificial flavors and colors, and that we're charged for those dubious additives besides.

I enjoy good food, and will take sufficient care to cook it well, but I won't take an undue amount of time. Most of the recipes for main meals take less than an hour to prepare. I think that's enough to invest in what could make or break your day. I depend on spices and condiments to vary what is sometimes a constant fare of hamburger or tuna, when nothing else can be found on the road.

Although I economize where possible, I don't begrudge paying for taste, quality, or nutrition. Food is the most important item for any active traveler. A bicyclist who pedals all day, a motorcyclist worn down from six hours of steady headwind, or a hitchhiker lugging a pack between rides at least deserves to eat well at night. To that proposition this cookbook is dedicated.

# Acknowledgments

Thanks are due to Clarke Bachman, who suggested I write the book, and Florence Queralt who corrected the manuscript.

# PART ONE

# GETTING ORGANIZED

# The Logistics
# of the Bike-Kitchen

I once knew a female biker who went on a long tour with just a one-quart pot and a can of sterno. She made lukewarm soups and weak cups of tea, and barely managed to warm food in cans. But she couldn't cook. That is, the woman didn't have the equipment with which to cook. She knew her way around the kitchen all right, but shortchanged herself on the road.

On another trip a bicyclist brought a 2½ pound stove, two large pots with lids, spices, condiments, and cooking ingredients, staples like sugar, raisins, and bread crumbs, and assorted utensils. At one time, the load totalled over twenty pounds. Considering that he carried fifty-five pounds of tent, sleeping bag, and other gear, it could have been a heavy load had the biker been alone. His situation was at the other extreme from the lightly-laden woman.

I was the second bicyclist. As it happened, I was traveling with a group of from four to eight riders around the perimeter of the United States. We shared the load on that "On the Edge of America" trip; a package of three to five pounds apiece was perfectly reasonable. By the end of the tour, the group dwindled to just me. By that time I had cut my gear to less than five pounds.

Those examples illustrate the range of possibilities when cooking on the road. A bicycle camper can choose some middle ground between the two. He may decide on a lightweight gasoline stove suitable for his needs, a small pot, and a few condiments and

3

supplies. When he travels with a few companions he might add more pots and accessories.

Well before the departure day for a tour arrives, the traveler should take stock of his needs and make a checklist. The list will not only remind him of what he lacks, should replace, or has almost run out of since the previous trip, but it also serves as an organizing device by which he can reassess his camping philosophy. Perhaps he needs a second stove, a light one using a convenient butane cartridge just for those short weekend trips. A two-pound teflon griddle may be worth the extra weight if he's with a large group and the others all like pancakes for breakfast.

The organizer of a tour should ask for suggested additions from the others to the checklist. Those who have camping experience would certainly add useful ideas, but even beginners have fresh thoughts and can indicate their food preferences and prejudices. Though no significant changes may result, the group participation brings about a feeling of cooperation and democratic choice. Often on past tours, when the going got tough and tempers became short, I'd be startled by a complaint like: "Why do we have so much cheese in our meals? I don't even like cheese." It's easier to avert that kind of conflict by compromise before the trip than to reconcile it in the middle of nowhere. And if irreconcilable differences do surface in the planning stage, some potential group members may decide not to come along after all. Better then than later. There's nothing as dispiriting to a group during a tour than seeing a member leaving it in a huff.

Here's a typical checklist, one I used for the "On the Edge of America" tour:

| | |
|---|---|
| gas stove, Phoebus 625 | long wooden spoon |
| fuel bottle, aluminum | measuring cup |
| simmering pad | measuring spoons |
| 3 quart pot | can opener |
| frypan or lid for pot | cooking glove |
| 6 quart kettle, lid | spices, in 35mm cans |
| clamping pot holder, aluminum | salt and pepper shakers |
| individual mess kits | liquid condiments |
| 6 inch knife, sheathed | cooking ingredients, dry |
| diamond-surfaced sharpener | plastic bottles |
| collapsible colander | plastic tubes |
| plastic spatula | 2½ gal. plastic water bag |

| | |
|---|---|
| 12 plastic food bags | matches |
| Ivory Snow flakes | 2 nylon net bags |
| plastic scouring pad | 15 ft. nylon cord |
| long-handled plastic brush | small flashlight |
| dish towel | candle lantern, folding |
| roll of toilet paper | candles |

You may disagree with this list. No doubt some of the items seem inessential while others are lacking. And that is precisely the import of a list. It's *your* evaluation of trip needs. My own list changes with each tour, because in some way—a change in the number of companions and their tastes, a different area to be visited or the length of the trip—each long ride is individual and its demands unique. I'd now add a wire whisk to the above list, for example, based on my last trip. I'd also skip shakers for salt and pepper, just keeping them in plastic bottles instead; I found that the top welded shut on the salt shaker. And I'd consider tongs if I were to fry a lot of chicken.

I find that it's a good idea to start putting together all my equipment some weeks before the tour. At first I just throw things into cardboard boxes as I think of them. At the same time, I think about and update my checklist, keeping it on my desk where I can always refer to it.

After a couple of weeks I compare the list to what's in the box. Invariably during those weeks, I remember things to add, make small changes, and buy needed items. No point in rushing about at the last minute! In the last few days before leaving I pack my panniers, organizing items by grouping them in plastic bags. On departure day I can feel assured I haven't forgotten anything.

A word of caution when gathering your touring equipment: don't raid your kitchen. Much domestic cookware is too cumbersome, heavy, or inadequate for camping. Often, pots and lids have grooves that are hard to wash out, or awkward handles that can't be removed. Specialized camping gear of good quality is the best choice. Besides, it's smarter to have your touring supplies complete and approximately ready to go independent of home needs. If you borrow freely between kitchen and camping gear you inevitably find yourself short of an item during a trip.

The first item on any cooking checklist—and the most important—is the stove. It's the most expensive single piece and the most indispensable. Unlike a utensil or a food, it can't be found just anywhere. The wrong choice of a stove, or lack of technique in using it, can mean hours of frustration. It's so crucial, in my view, that I devote a whole chapter to the stove and its operation.

Next to consider is the kind of container in which you plan to cook. It's not a simple decision. A number of factors pertain: the container's size, weight, durability and cost, its ability to heat evenly, non-stickiness, and even whether it can be carried easily on the bike or in a pack.

The ideal pot, pan, or skillet would be lightweight, yet thick-walled and able to transmit heat evenly to the food. It would fit inside of a pannier bag without straining it, and yet be large enough to boil spaghetti for a group. That pot would also last almost forever, be easily washed, and reasonable in cost.

Such a pot doesn't exist, of course. When you gain one feature you lose another. With a light pot, food sticks and the metal itself gets distorted from the heat. A large one has to be carried gypsy-like outside of the packs. A decent non-stick surface is expensive. The best the road-camper can do is compromise among the factors and choose what is important to him, be it cost, weight, or quality.

You can use more than one container, of course, each for a particular purpose. Overall weight would be increased, but you'd have more convenience. Separate dishes could be cooked, and smaller pots do fit more easily into packs. With a larger group, a second or even third container would probably be a necessity. You simply would need the greater volume to produce enough food for all. One large kettle might cook the pasta for six people, for example, while a smaller one would produce the main meat dish. Those two could even be supplemented by a non-stick frying pan, either as an extra pan or main container for broiled dishes.

A number of manufacturers make cookware especially for campers. Among them are Mirro, Palco, Hope, and Sigg. Two design features distinguish camping cookware from what is found in the ordinary kitchen: lightness and compactness. Most of the material used in those containers is thin, stamped aluminum. A two-quart pot typically weighs 3/4 pound, and a four-quart slightly over a pound. Some lids are also touted as frying pans, but this is a poor practice. Their thinness causes sticking and burning, and they warp easily. Some manufacturers roll the edges of their containers, which helps prevent warping a bit.

Cast aluminum is more durable, but it has the same drawbacks if the walls are thin. Stainless steel is of still better quality, but unless it has a bottom specially designed for heat distribution, it also suffers from hot spots. With each step upward in quality, you pay more.

Compactness is achieved by "nesting" a set of pots within each other so that the overall size is of the largest pot. In addition, wire handles—or flat metal handles in the case of frypans—swing out of the way when not in use. The usual cover has a D-ring and is flat; you can keep a cooked dish warm on it while making the next.

All cookware manufacturers supply complete sets. These are a better bargain, but you may be buying some items you don't need. Individual kits, or mess kits, contain a plate, frypan, cup, and small pot, and cost less than $10. They weigh under a pound, but are next to useless for serious touring. The handles pull out at the rivets and about all you can cook without burning are liquid types of dishes.

There's no escaping weight as the most important factor in selecting cookware. Only a thicker wall and bottom, regardless of material, will heat evenly and keep its shape over the years. Obviously, an extremely heavy object such as a cast iron skillet should not be taken on a two-wheel trip. But one of a heavy-weight, cast aluminum would be a good compromise.

Both manufacturers and retailers seem reluctant to quantify the thickness of their products. They describe them in such glowing sales terms as heavy duty, sturdy lightweight, or thicker weight. Salesmen are of little help, in most cases just reading the labels for the customer, as if he or she were illiterate. The only retailer I found who specifies thickness is Sears Roebuck. Its catalog lists cookware as either eighteen gauge or the thicker twelve gauge. In the absence of such data, the buyer can measure the pot himself or weigh it. Everything else being equal, the more the weight and the thicker the material, the greater the worth.

Exactly how much extra do you carry when you opt for a heavier gauge? A two-quart pot in eighteen gauge aluminum, without cover, weighs nine ounces, compared to fifteen ounces in twelve gauge. Comparisons in other sizes would be proportionate. The weight penalty doesn't seem excessive. Personally, I'd rather carry those additional ounces than struggle with a lighter but inferior product. Save those ounces somewhere else—by leaving home a pair of extra shoes, for example, or reducing your own body weight.

More and more cookware today is made with various non-stick surfaces. Among those, in ascending order of quality and cost, are Teflon, Silverstone, and T-Fal. These surface treatments are especially valuable in frying pans, but they're also useful in pots and griddles. Although the greatest percentage of on-road recipes are of the liquid or casserole type, many of the combined meat and pasta or rice dishes are apt to stick. With a non-stick surface you don't have to be as careful to stir frequently, and clean-up is easier.

None of those surfaces stand rugged treatment; they should only be touched by wood or plastic. On a general principle of safety first, I always tuck a non-stick pan into a nylon bag, into which I place only plastic articles. I never allow any metal object to be used near that surface. No matter how carefully you may handle a fork or a spoon in such a pan, slight nicks and scratches inevitably result. They soon build up and the surface becomes useless.

Teflon tends to get scratched quite easily. Even in the store, you can find scratches in cookware just from normal customer handling. The problem is even more acute in touring. Silverstone, a Du Pont surface process, is more rugged. The company claims it to be some thirty to fifty percent thicker. Its instructions caution you to avoid sudden changes of temperature nevertheless. With care, this surface should serve you well.

T-Fal is mechanically bonded to the base metal itself; it gives the most protection and can stand up to the most rugged use. A much higher cost is due partly to the fact that it's imported from France. A cheaper version using the same type of treatment, with the acronym PTFE, is sold by Sears in a whole line of sizes. I've found no apparent differences between the two in actual use.

As of this writing, unfortunately, cookware designed specifically for camping is not available in T-Fal, and Silverstone is found only on some frying pans. That shouldn't deter you. There is no reason that regular kitchen pots coated with these surfaces couldn't be used. The only possible difficulty would be the plastic handles. Many of these are attached with a bolt, which can be removed and a clamping pot holder used instead. But I've found that a fixed handle is not too awkward to pack if you choose compatible sizes of pot and pannier. Take your carrying bag into the store to see how it will fit.

Unlike camping gear, which can be hung on the outside of bike packs by wire handles, kitchen pots would have to be packed in your pannier bags. Until camping cookware is made in heavier aluminum and with the new surfaces, the only way you can get a quality product is to buy it in a kitchen appliance outlet instead of a camping store, notwithstanding the lack of such features as wire handles and flat lids.

How do you select a pot or frypan from among the many available? How do you judge various characteristics in dozens of products? It's not easy. Much depends on how much you want to pay or carry, what use you'll put it to, and how often you plan to use it.

It's even hard to decide what type of pot to use if there's only one or two riders. Should it be a skillet perhaps? As well as frying in it, you can make one-pot dinners also. But you couldn't boil pasta easily in such a shallow container. A two- or three-quart pot would be better for that purpose. You'd forego frying in those, however. And so the arguments go. There just isn't one universally acknowledged best piece of cookware.

Still, something must be picked. When alone, for a short tour, my choice is a simple mess kit, nesting together a deep plate, frypan, cup, and 3/4 quart pot. Its only virtues are the light weight and the compactness. The kit suffices for a week's worth of soups, chili, and franks and beans.

In the past, with one or two others, I used a three-quart, eighteen gauge aluminum pot, with a lid that doubled as my personal plate. The pot and cover weighed just eleven ounces. I could make rice or pasta for three, or a one-pot meal for four in that pot. But meat would stick while browning, unless it was drowned in oil and stirred frequently. Since the one-pot meals that we made contained enough of a liquid base, I wasn't too concerned about sticking or uneven heating.

The other group members brought the plates or mess kits of their choice. The kits were useful when making dinner; they served as additional containers for preparing vegetables, heating water for coffee, and various other uses.

With a larger group I added a six-quart kettle. We took one on our USA trip. There were enough of us to justify the extra weight: Dennis Devlin and Clarke Bachman of Philadelphia; Maureen Bonness, Naples, Florida; Jim Born, Indianapolis; Bonnie Wong, Oakland, California; Myke Dickey, San Diego, and others who joined for short stretches. With the addition of an auxiliary stove as a second burner, we were able to cook almost anything we wanted.

Today, I'd probably bring either a nine- or ten-inch, twelve-gauge skillet, one with straight sides instead of the omelet type. Either a Silverstone surface, such as is used in the Wear-Ever line, or the Sears PTFE would do. The ten-inch Wear-Ever has a capacity of 2 1/2 quarts and a weight of 1 1/2 pounds. A cover would add half a pound, but that weight and bulk can be saved by using aluminum foil instead, pressed over the sides or tied with the bike's elastic straps; and the handle can be removed to save a few more ounces.

The Sears ten-inch, PTFE-coated cake pan, without a handle, weighs just half a pound. Its thin metal would seem unsuitable for frying, but it shouldn't warp if the flame is never turned up higher than medium. At least it hasn't for me so far, over a short period of use.

The choice of a skillet depends on the other members' food preferences—whether frying was important to them—and their willingness to carry it as an extra piece. But I believe a skillet to be a good choice even as main container for two or three; a smaller one could do for a lone traveler. In addition to fried and braised dishes, many one-pot dishes could be made in it.

No matter what the size of the group, I'd never take what I consider the sheer luxuries of cooking gear: a coffee pot, pressure cooker, griddle, foldable grate, or folding oven either (the kind that is placed over a stove). Even if compact, an oven is an awkward item at best, not fitting into any pannier and hard to strap on the packs. Its use conflicts with the rest of the meal preparation, increasing time substantially. If the riders want a break from bakery bread, there are always quick breads that can be made in a frying pan.

Something we did find handy during our United States trip, although not indispensable, was a collapsible colander. Clarke suggested it after burning his fingers a couple of times. Carrying that additional seven ounces may seem like sheer extravagance, in the face of agonizing over the weight of pots. But if boiled pasta in all its forms is important in your cuisine, the colander makes life much easier. There's nothing as frustrating as trying to drain a hot kettle full of thin spaghetti, without losing a fourth of it. You can also steam vegetables and clams with it (see "Traveling Without Meat," pg. 137), and rinse vegetables and fruit in it over a sink. In the evening it can be a popcorn maker.

A proper, sharp knife makes meal preparation safer and simpler. Don't buy either a Bowie knife or a penknife, or even one of those Swiss Army marvels. On our last trip, Jim Born kept a foot-long bayonet-like knife strapped to his hip. I constantly anticipated the police picking him up for carrying a dangerous weapon.

Use only one knife for food, ideally with a blade about six inches long and in the shape of a chef knife. If nothing else, it'll make you feel like the chef that you aspire to be. The knife you'd want is a compromise between the heavy meat-cutter and the thinner paring knife. Don't practice knife throwing with it; use the Bowie knife instead, if you can't resist that sport to amuse yourself. No whittling either, which can be better done with the Swiss knife.

Rather than carry a heavy sharpening stone, buy a lightweight, diamond surface sharpener. The only manufacturer I know that makes them is EZE-LAP. Its excellent "backpacker" model weighs just two ounces, with case, and gives many years of service. Sharpening a knife with it takes less than a minute and you can hone the blade nightly in seconds to keep a razor edge. Another version, an oversized nail file that weighs an ounce, can also double as a maintenance tool to remove burrs from rough spots on bike or equipment.

The use of other utensils and accessories on my checklist are mostly self-evident. Some can be eliminated by diehards who'd want to save every bit of weight. As examples: You could double a dish towel as a cooking glove—and your personal bath towel for both. The spatula could do for a wooden spoon. And it could be argued that you don't even need a fork if you have a spoon. That's the way most Asians, and many Europeans, eat their meals.

Striving for ounce-saving can get you into trouble sometimes. You may not be able to reach the bottom of the pot with a spatula, for instance. A measuring cup can double as a drinking cup, but not when it's coated with the cooking oil you just measured out! And if it's made of metal, it'll burn your lips. A ceramic cup would be the most comfortable choice, if you can stand the extra ounces. It's best to think through the purpose of each item you take.

The value of other equipment is not always obvious. A water container may seem a luxury on first thought, for example. Those with experience in state parks or rustic sites can appreciate, however, that water is often far from the cooking area. It could be brought over in your pot, of course, but what do you do with it when you have to use the pot for cooking? The amount that you can store in bike bottles is negligible for your cooking, drinking, and washing needs. To walk constantly back and forth to your water source is a nuisance.

Some camps—in forests, beaches, or primitive sites in National Parks and Forests—don't even have water, and you'd need to bring it in. A container would be an absolute necessity then. The plastic one that I carry with groups collapses to 9 x 11 inches and a thickness of an inch or so, and weighs just six ounces.

Soft-walled plastic tubes are the best containers for "wet" foods such as peanut butter, ketchup, or mustard. After squeezing out the last of the contents, toothpaste-like, the tubes are refilled from the bottom by removing a clip. They last forever, are very light, and are also good for sugar, coffee, flour, and other powdery ingredients.

Plastic is one of the most practical materials a road-camper has, in fact. He uses a large sheet of it for a moisture-proof ground cover and to save wear on the tent or sleeping bag. Some tourers won't use a tent at all. They hang a temporary sheet of plastic overhead in case of rain. Plastic bags keep clothes clean and dry within nylon panniers, which are generally only semiwaterproof. It's a wonder how early pioneers got along without this modern material. The only thing they had was oil cloth, a messy alternative indeed.

For cooking purposes, plastic bags help organize groups of utensils, condiments, and staples. It's easier to find a can opener or matches within an accessory bag than loose in a pannier. That kind of organization enables the weight of the load to be distributed evenly among group members, too. I weigh each bag's contents and make note of it. As the group changes in composition, it's easy to reshuffle the bags among the members equitably.

You can mix salads in the bags, as well as dredge meat with flour. Plastic helps hold in the scent of stored foods and minimizes midnight raids by raccoons, chipmunks, and mice, not to mention bears. Don't depend on only plastic to keep away animals though. Place food in plastic, within net bags, and hang it by a rope from a branch of a tree. A caution however: choose plastic that is safe for food. Some are meant for storing goods or garbage only.

It's a good idea to place all containers holding liquids into two plastic bags and to twist-tie them well, to prevent calamities in case of breakage or leaks. The kind to use is the heavy freeze-bag. As the bags become dirty or worn they find a last use as garbage containers.

Stiff-walled, polyethylene bottles are lightweight and come with non-leak, wide-mouth caps. About the only liquid I couldn't keep from seeping out of them, for some reason, was soy sauce. The wide mouth of these bottles allows easy spooning when measuring dry ingredients. Bottles made of nalgene, a high density polyethylene, are easier to clean and less likely to absorb odors.

Spices need a special mention. When touring with a large group, I've carried twenty-six spices, besides eight liquid ingredients such as soy, tabasco, oil, honey, and even a bit of cooking wine. Dennis made a sport of bringing the bag of spices into a restaurant where we'd be eating to match spices with the cook. The cook usually lost on the third or fourth match, at tarragon or maybe curry powder.

The spices, kept in half-full 35mm cans, weighed only about a pound. The variety of taste made possible by spices makes them worth twice that weight. Food in remote stores is often limited to tuna or packaged sausage, and even hamburger and chicken get monotonous if plainly cooked. Rice, bland when used alone, takes on a dozen different flavors with spices.

Now that you've chosen and gotten all your equipment together, how do you carry it on the bike? I'm not concerned here with load balancing and distribution. That's quite important and can affect the way any two-wheeled vehicle handles, and even its safety. Those factors should get first priority. Within those constraints, though, you do have a choice of how to pack your cooking gear.

Some tourers don't especially care where they put everything. A little thought will show that one place is not just as good as another. Take the case of your leftover staples, for instance. If you hadn't finished some meat or a bit of cheese, or want to carry a ripe piece of fruit for a snack later or the next day, where would you pack it? Certainly not in the upper portion of your pannier bag where the sun can bake it. A super-heated banana or peach oozes like syrup among the bag's contents.

The same is true for spices, which deteriorate with heat. You'd want to put those perishables deeper into the bag, under an insulating layer of clothes or covered by a loaf of bread. I find that the middle of my bag stays cool for hours, even on the hottest days. Whole gingerroot stored there, for example, stays fresh until used up.

In addition to using insulation, I make a point of packing my food on the side away from the expected direction of the sun. So if I'm traveling in a general westward direction, I pack food on the northern, right side of the bike, away from the direct rays of the sun. On the way back I shift the food to the other side.

Rugged or soft items, such as a plastic water container, a frying pan, or a towel, may be stored in the outer parts of the pack where they can contribute to physical protection. A big pot is best not packed inside at all. If it has a wire handle, it can be stuck over the end of a sleeping bag or tent roll on the back of the bike. If not, it can be tied by an elastic strap on top of the packs.

The stove—bulky and often quite dirty—is best kept separate, at least in a plastic bag or its own stuff sack. On a bicycle, I find that a front pannier bag, which has a low center of gravity and is of about the right size, can hold the stove and spares, as well as a tool kit. The spare fuel bottle fits snugly into a standard water bottle fixture. I mount this very low on the bicycle, near the bottom bracket on the underside of the down tube. There it's completely out of the way and can't contaminate anything in case of spillage. I never pack it inside a pannier. It should be mounted on the outside of motorized two-wheel vehicles, too.

You should organize the packing of kitchen equipment in the panniers. A discussion of the brands available and their features is beyond the scope of this book, but I offer a couple of suggestions. Choose panniers with a large capacity and with a few outside pockets. The difference in price is worth it, if only to have room for those extras that you inevitably collect. Among the large ones are Kangaroo and Kirtland.

I prefer rear panniers that tie with a drawstring at the top, in the manner of a duffel bag. A cover flap ties down over it to provide a double thickness of rain protection. That enables you to pack the contents tightly and allows for expansion as you add things to the bag. Kirtland and Karrimor (British make) are the only two brands I know with this design. Kirtland's bag also has a pouch built into the cover, an extra bonus.

It's best to reserve either a whole pannier, or most of one, for kitchen equipment. Place heavy items in the bottom: the stove (if it's not in a front pannier), and a package of "wet" condiments. Those would be liquids in plastic bottles, such as honey, soy sauce, oil, and syrup. I wedge five or six of those bottles tightly into a five-inch pot, without a handle. A two pound coffee can, cut down, does as well. Or if you carry more bottles you can buy REI's aluminum provision box, measuring about eight by five by two inches, or a plastic refrigerator container.

Put that whole containerful of condiments, bottles upright, inside a sturdy plastic bag, and let it sit square and level on the bottom of the bag. The elaborate precautions are worth it. I found out the hard way that plastic bottles inevitably leak, no matter how secure the tops. Oil and syrup spilled in a bag can be a real mess. But inside the double safeguard of pot and plastic, a leak can be contained.

Over this base of stove and condiments I pack a plastic bag full of polyethylene tubes containing dry condiments: sugar, coffee, or flour. Alongside, on the same level, goes a bagful of accessories and utensils, such as a can opener, knife, sharpener, and measuring cup and spoons. As can be seen, everything is organized into small groups of related items and packed in plastic bags. But the spatula, wooden spoon, and cleaning brush are too long to fit easily in a bag, and I keep them loose anywhere in that area.

Before packing further, I stand the simmering pad against the back of the pannier. If there's a frying pan, I make a package of that, filling it with my mess kit plate and the package of utensils, and place all in a snug stuff sack. Then I place it against the simmering pad in the back, or against the outside of the pannier wall. The bagful of spices and any perishables are next, about in the middle of the pannier. To insulate those further, the cooking glove, towel (if dry; if not, strapped outside) and the balance of the equipment, as well as the store of dry cereal, is piled over them.

Certain items should be kept in the panniers' outside pockets, where they can be reached easily. Net bags are necessary for shopping, toilet paper has uses other than in the kitchen, the flashlight and lantern may be needed before cooking starts. You shouldn't have to grope for them in a pannier when you want them. The main cooking pot, as mentioned before, is strapped on the outside.

If there's still room in the bag—there probably is if you bought a large one—pack your "evening" or special clothes last. That would include a nylon jacket, leg warmers, sweater, rain gear, and gloves. They're the things you're likely to need in the cool of the evening or in case of rain. Don't use the space for any of your "change" clothes, for bike tools or spares, writing material, or other non-cooking items. When you set up for supper, you wouldn't want to unpack those items needlessly and have them strewn out. Best to keep them in the other pannier, according to their own organizational scheme.

As the load of equipment grows larger with more riders, there's a chance that a group may disagree about who should carry what. The easiest way to defuse that issue is to let each person select his share of weight among a number of packaged units of the equipment. A share is determined by the number of people. I keep the weight of the packages about a pound each, convenient for suitable distribution; I carry what is left over. I find little argument with this system.

A last thought about equipment: who should own it all? I found the question crucial on an overseas trip of mine. My companion owned almost all the cooking gear. Well into the tour, at a time and place where it was impossible to buy replacements, we decided to separate. He took it all, of course. I had only my mess kit and no place to buy a stove or pot. After that, I was obliged to eat all meals in restaurants. I didn't mind—the cost was low and the food good—but it would have made me feel better if I had the option of making meals.

Now I always make sure that the cooking equipment is mine. If not, for some reason, I have a stove and gear at home ready to be mailed to me. Should a problem arise, I'd have the means to continue alone with just a short mailing delay. Others might feel more secure in bringing along a second, personal set. Unfortunately, that defeats the advantage of sharing the weight of equipment among many.

# Let's Go Shopping

At a small grocery in Indus, Minnesota I asked for cheese. "All we have is this big package of Velveeta," the woman told me. She showed me the five pound brick.

"I only need a few slices to use in a casserole," I said.

I was about to give up, but after a bit of friendly conversation the woman said, "Oh, what the heck. I'll just cut off a little for you." When I objected—admittedly only mildly—she answered that what she couldn't sell she'd take home and eat herself.

The incident illustrates both the problems faced and the flexibility that is possible when shopping in rural areas. Their grocery stock increasingly comes from national distributors, with most foods packaged in standard units. The seller of a large brick of cheese assumes you have a refrigerator to keep it in and a family-sized group to consume it. Even fruit is cellophaned in six-packs.

On the other hand, the rural grocery still remains informal. Owners will split packages and will even sell you something out of their own, often adjoining homes. Many times I've been sold, or simply given, a vegetable or two, a handful of nuts, or a few slices of bread. In foreign countries, and occasionally in America, an owner will open his closed store to accommodate a bicyclist. The sight of you on a bike no doubt strikes a sympathetic chord in the natives, whose routine is often livened by your unorthodox arrival. It all comes with the adventure and joy of two-wheel travel.

Besides the small village store and the obvious supermarket, other sources of food are farmers and private homes. They might sell not only produce from roadside stands, but eggs, dressed poultry and honey, and an assortment of home-baked pies and cakes. The vegetables and fruit available "privately" are almost always of better quality than store-bought, since they are tree ripened and fresh. Jams and jellies from such sources are pure and delicious. If you notice a private home with a garden, try it for produce even if there's no stand. You'll at least get some conversation if you can't buy anything.

Stores in campgrounds are expensive and have limited fare as a rule, but they're a handy source of milk and bulky, hard-to-carry items. You can buy or cadge food in emergencies from churches, schools, remote ranches, or work gangs in lumber or railroad camps. Even restaurants can be sources of staples. I've often replenished small amounts of salt, sugar, or spices from their kitchens.

Some road-campers subscribe to a system of making up small packages of dry ingredients at home, each exactly enough to cook one meal. They carry enough of these packages to last the trip. It saves time on the road, and is fine for a short outing with one or two people. When touring national parks or remote areas, prepackaged meals that are ready for the pot may be easier than searching for a store.

But ordinarily, there's little to be gained from prepackaging for a group of four or five on a longer trip. Two weeks worth of those packets would be quite a load. Also, a large group is usually able to use up most of the bulk ingredients that it buys in one or two meals. Some staples are always carried, of course. A suggested list of those and of condiments is given in the appendix.

In addition to staples, the group should have emergency rations set aside. These should be light and compact foods, such as dried soups, sardines, or tuna. A good choice also is beef jerky. It's best for each member to fend for himself here, placing some reserve food deep in his pack for that lean time. Tastes vary, and the biker may even be separated from the others sometimes.

Most travelers—pedal and motorized both—overprepare themselves for emergencies. There is no need for more than one day's worth. The staples you carry, although not imaginative, would keep you from starving. You're never completely surprised by desolation in a given area, in any case, being warned by people or by indications on the map.

Since shopping is normally done at the end of the riding day, not far from camp, the food you buy can be the ordinary, off-shelf kind with no concern for weight or size. Contrary to most bikers' expectations, the kind of food most appropriate on tour is not the freeze-dried, backpacking type.

It's expensive, in the first place. And it's not very appetizing, even when eaten by active travelers. Why anyone would buy freeze-dried spaghetti, for example, is beyond me. Dry pasta is cheap, light, and easily prepared. A pack of spaghetti sauce mix from a supermarket is surely as light as the freeze-dried kind, if that were the sole issue. Your homemade spaghetti can be prepared to suit your taste and its texture will have substance, rather than be a mush. The same can be said of other dehydrated meats and vegetables, most of which have the same baby food consistency when cooked. I prefer to bite into my beans and celery.

Most of the time, the groups of which I was a part didn't make any provision for lunch, letting each person do what he would. Our riding styles were individual and the group didn't necessarily stick together during the day. When two or more wanted to share makings for lunch, that was up to them. I usually had peanut butter and jelly sandwiches, cheese, and fruit.

Our group would make a practice of fixing the day's rendezvous point at the last known grocery store before the riding objective. We would ask ahead for the store's location and hours of operation. A telephone call to the store would be worth the cost, even if from twenty or thirty miles away. You'd take a chance on it being closed on arrival, or might shop needlessly ahead of time, and why carry that food for all those miles?

A shopping stop was always an exciting time. The riding was virtually over for the day, we were all together again, and it was happy hour.

Our pack-laden bikes outside a small-town store advertised our presence. Our bizarre appearance invited questions. On our United States trip Clarke would stand nonchalantly, with chin beard and helmet, a rear view mirror attached to its side, looking like a man from outer space to the locals. Kids gathered—"You in a race, mister?"—and shoppers stopped to talk. Once we were approached by a farmer's wife and invited to camp at "an honest-to-goodness farm." Another time, a very old man shuffled up to me and put a quarter in my palm, saying very pleasantly, "Here sonny, this is for you."

Inside the store, conduct should be more businesslike. One or two of the group do the actual shopping—they have the cooking duty that day—and make the decisions that will affect the gastronomic well-being of the rest an hour or two later.

You should buy economically. Some principles will be discussed in a later chapter on costs, but a methodical approach helps: this means a shopping list. As the cook runs out of ingredients day by day, he or she adds those to the list, as well as the shopping suggestions of others. The cookbook or recipe should be taken to the store to make sure that no needed items are overlooked.

The rest should leave the shoppers alone. The time to make suggestions is prior to entering the store; a crowd just makes shopping take longer. It probably irritates the proprietor, too, and there's no use in antagonizing him; he might well be helpful in supplying information and perhaps accommodating the group's shopping needs.

The evening's menu may be determined before shopping, but what you cook is often the result of what's available in the store. In a large town or city there's no problem. You're able to revel in exotic dishes, perhaps lobster on the Northeast coast or shrimp jambalaya in a Gulf fishing port. But in a Montana village, the only food source may be a combination gas station and convenience food mart. You might then have a choice of franks or bacon as your meat entree. If lucky, you might find some frozen hamburger that could thaw between store and camp. If there's nothing else, you may have to resort to the one standby available in any store in America, canned tuna. In the absence of fresh vegetables in the store, you'd depend on your onion flakes and some canned peas or tomato to make a meal with that tuna.

A road traveler soon learns that he doesn't first consult his cookbook in a small store. Instead he goes to the refrigerated section and determines what he has to settle for. Only then does he search in his cookbook for recipes that are possible with the available meat, eggs, or cheese. Possible, because he must also find the other foods to support the menu. As the very last resort, he might have to give up and buy canned beef stew or canned spaghetti— ugh! Occasionally, the group will discuss the horrible options; they may decide to chuck it all and eat at the local cafe.

Those are the dark moments. We won't dwell on them. For such lean times, I offer recipes that make use of franks, canned meats, and other convenient foods. With spices, rice, and different kinds of dehydrated flakes, they make a passable meal. Spices, for me, make almost anything tolerable.

How much food should you buy for the evening meal? From past experience my rough estimate is that a quart of cooked food, by volume, is needed to satisfy an active bicyclist. Other less active travelers may need less.

Nutrition aside, there's no question in my mind that most of that volume should be in the form of carbohydrates. You need them to pedal all day. Dr. Kenneth Cooper of *Aerobics* fame estimates that 300 or more calories per hour are burned when bicycling vigorously. For six or seven hours, that adds up to 2,000 calories above what is needed in a sedentary person's diet.

Proportionately less protein would be needed. Consequently, the recipes in this cookbook call for less meat in relation to starches and vegetables. I base each recipe on four to six ounces of meat, without bone, per person. Fish and chicken are increased a bit, to one-third or a half pound per biker. For the volume ingested, that's a small amount of protein. Some more of it is supplied through cheese, other milk products, and legumes. Should anyone feel undernourished on that quantity of protein, he can increase the amount of meat in the recipe.

Volume is supplied by classical meat extenders: vegetables, rice, pasta, beans, eggs, and cheeses. Starches can be calculated on a basis of 1½ cups, cooked, per person. About the same amount of cooked cereal would do for breakfast. The rest of the volume is supplied by bread, liquid portions of the meal, and dessert.

Individuals differ in their needs, of course. Jim Born ate unbelievable amounts during our "Edge" trip, well beyond the quart of an average biker. I was convinced he could have eaten the contents of the whole pot if he had set his mind to it. Others, with a lower rate of metabolism, needed less.

The food allotted per serving by most cookbooks would not suffice for hungry bikers. You'd have to increase it by fifty percent at least. I've tried to calculate a realistic volume for active travelers in my recipes.

If the shopper wants to halve or double a recipe, he simply amends it to that degree and buys accordingly. The principle doesn't hold precisely—to double a recipe that calls for browning onions wouldn't necessarily mean doubling the amount of oil too, but it's a close enough rule of thumb.

Once the shopping is done, all share in the additional burden of carrying the groceries into camp. The extra weight is hardly ever more than a few pounds apiece for a few miles. Room can always be found for food, whether inside packs or strapped outside. Such crushables as bread or marshmallows can be carried in nylon bags, dangling from the top of the packs. Frozen items that need thawing should be exposed to the sun. By the time you're ready to cook, they'll be soft enough.

I've always placed milk securely inside a pannier, usually in my front one where I could watch it. Eggs were cushioned in some clothes in my handlebar bag, after I temporarily removed the two small cameras I usually had there. Some people simply break eggs into a jar, ready for scrambling or an omelet.

Be careful of spills and breakage in bike bags, especially because of the scent left behind. That goes for any unwrapped food too, even such seemingly innocuous items like nuts or apples. Maureen had her bag mauled by a raccoon in Maine—no food was in it at the time but the smell was—and once before, in India, varmints ate right through my tent wall and a pannier bag, heading straight to a few peanut shells that were left in one of the bag's pockets.

# That Capricious One-Burner

Most non-campers romanticize mealtimes in the open. They imagine themselves before a crackling fire, a caldron set on forked sticks, the gurgling of a nearby brook, and companions sitting raptly in a circle toasting marshmallows and spinning stories.

Writers of camping books contribute to this mystique. They describe hot-rocks and foil cooking, tell how to forage for wild spices in the woods, and they even include the words and music of songs to sing around the fire. All nonsense, relating to the macho instinct and primitive urges.

For me a campfire evokes other excitements: popping sparks that sting hands and singe clothes and hair; the soft firelight that strains the ability to read a recipe; the dubious fun of starting a flame in a downpour (and where do you find forked sticks in a desert or plain?) and the taste of scorched marshmallows.

To paraphrase Dorothy Parker, Coleman is quicker. And much simpler and convenient. There's no need of a whole crew seeking firewood using a stove, no coaxing a flame, no choking in pungent smoke. Not that a stove is without shortcomings. But on balance, I'd lean to the compact backpacker stove every time.

Such a stove is cheaper in the first place. Wood just doesn't lie around for the taking, and if it does, dozens of other campers see it well before you ever arrive at the site. You have to buy wood nowadays, for anywhere from fifty cents to three dollars an armful. That dampens the romance of a fire somewhat. A day's worth of gasoline costs twenty cents or so, about twelve cents for an hour of burning time.

Adjusting the position of a pot into and out of a fire to control its heat is a constant chore. The flames blacken its bottom terribly. The last straw is that in many parks and forests, open fires are not permitted at all.

The so-called backpacker stove—it also serves bicyclists, motorcyclists, mopeders, and other road travelers splendidly—comes in various designs, and it uses any of a half dozen fuels. As with cooking pots, there is no one best stove. Each has its advantages and shortcomings, and you should choose the one that best suits your particular needs.

There are stoves that you fill with liquid fuel: white gas, kerosene, alcohol, and a few others not so readily available. These fuels must be vaporized under pressure to be burned. The chamber of the stove is often primed, or preheated, by burning some fuel on its outside. Many stoves have built-in pumps to pressurize the fuel chamber, although a few need neither pumping nor priming. Once the stove warms up, you pump it infrequently, if at all, and its own heat vaporizes the fuel.

White gas, or the Coleman or Blazo equivalent, is the most popular fuel for these stoves. It has the highest heat output, and the stove can be primed with a bit of the same gas.

The liquid fuel stove can be bought anywhere in America. Unfortunately, the fuel is often not available in convenient amounts for lightly-laden travelers. Almost no store will sell you a pint of Coleman or Blazo, which come in gallon containers only. Those are too heavy (eight lbs.) and awkward to take on a moped or bicycle, although motorcyclists may find room for them. You can sometimes buy a pint's worth from a camper in an RV, or from the owner of the campground, but I wouldn't count on it.

The white gas of yesteryear that was sold at gas stations everywhere is no more, alas. The unleaded gas of today contains additives which clog the stoves. Most white gas models come with a warning not to use no-lead gas. But you can live with that automotive gas and the occasional maintenance in some stoves, as I'll discuss later.

Although they have almost as high heat output as white gas models, kerosene stoves are less popular. The fuel's odor offends many people. When kerosene spills it evaporates slowly, and the smell is persistent. It even sticks with you after washing.

Kerosene isn't sold as universally as gas in the United States, at least not in bulk at gas stations. In rural areas it's sometimes sold from barrels in hardware stores, as well as at gas stations. Otherwise it comes in gallon cans. You can't prime this stove with its own fuel, at least not easily. Ian Hibell, the well-known bicycle tourer, uses kerosene as a primer according to Josh Lehman, who rode with him in Scandinavia. But the fuel is not volatile enough to light readily. Alcohol or gas has to be carried for preheating.

Kerosene is a good choice for travel in Europe and Asia, where it's sold everywhere while gas may be scarce. Kerosene, because it's not as flammable as gasoline, presents no danger of flare or explosion. And it's the cheapest fuel—about three cents an hour of burning time.

Few campers use alcohol—at least not in their stoves. It's cost for stove use is as high as in a barroom shot glass. Although no priming is required and it evaporates quickly when spilled, alcohol has a low heat output. It also takes two to three times as long to bring a quart of water to boil as in a gas stove. This kind of stove is a poor buy.

And yet, some campers swear by it. Mike Hyman, who lives and climbs in northern Sweden, says that the Trangia alcohol stove is popular among backpackers in that country. Mike is surprised that the stove isn't better known in America. Although this stove is not very hot, it burns cleanly, needs no maintenance, simmers well, and uses fuel that is sold in convenient one-liter cans, at least in Sweden. Perhaps I'll try it on my next long trip.

In addition to stoves with liquid fuels, there are also those which use replaceable fuel cartridges. Their compressed gas—propane, butane, or liquid petroleum (LP)—is ready almost instantly for use at its highest capacity. Such stoves provide the utmost in simplicity: no smells, priming, or preheating. They are popular with the casual camper who'd rather not chant incantations over a tricky stove to make a cup of tea.

However, you pay for this convenience heavily in fuel efficiency and cost. Cartridge stoves compare favorably with those using white gas in the time needed to bring water to boil, at sea level and normal temperatures. With increases in altitude their efficiency decreases faster than white gas models. At temperatures below freezing, LP stoves take twice as long to reach a boil as at 60°F; some never do. At low temperatures butane is next to useless, although propane is not affected.

Another disadvantage of cartridge stoves is that as cartridges are used up their pressure goes down and so does their efficiency, to one half or less. Once fitted into the stove, butane cartridges cannot be removed until used up; you have to take along the partial one. LP and propane can be removed. None of the backpack types of cartridges are refillable, and you'd be obliged to bring a supply along if you're in an area where they're scarce. One propane cartridge weighs 1.8 pounds, a heavy burden for a bicyclist or someone on foot, but motorized travelers may not mind it.

Burning at a maximum flame for ninety minutes to three hours, a butane cartridge costs close to $1.50, six to ten times an hour as much as white gas. A propane cartridge costs more initially but lasts longer. Its cost per hour is about that of butane, a little less with some brands of stoves. The Primus Grasshopper, for example, burns at a simmer for eight hours at about twenty-five cents an hour. It may be just the thing for a motorcyclist or car owner, with its fuss-free operation, simplicity, and moderate cost.

Bender Hash of Salt Lake City, a hiker and hunter, suggests a few advantages of the cartridge over gas stoves that may not be immediately obvious. He points out that a cartridge stove can be easily turned off, even for short intervals, between burnings. By contrast the gas stove wastes fuel in that respect, needs more time to warm up after starting, and spills fuel more easily. It's not as safe as a cartridge either. Hash favors the Gaz-Bluet butane except in cold weather, for which he uses the Svea 123 gas stove.

Many users would agree with Hash. My feeling is that gas cartridge stoves are all right for trips of two or three days, but you'd have to discount them for long tours, except as second stoves or back-ups. The choice for a distance traveler usually narrows down to a white gas stove, at least in the United States. Kerosene is a strong competitor overseas.

Because of their popularity, more white gas stoves are made than all other stoves combined. Their efficiency may differ by a factor of two, but that isn't the sole basis on which to pick one over the other. You'd also want to consider a stove's weight and size, its sturdiness and ability to hold a simmer, the fuel tank capacity and burning time, cold weather use, maintenance needs, and its built-in features—pump, cleaning needle, or windshield.

Stove weights vary from about a pound for the MSR-GK to three-and-a-half pounds for the Optimus 111B (all weights are given without fuel or fuel bottle). Typical stoves weigh about one-and-a-half pounds—the popular Svea 123 is 17 ounces and the Phoebus 725 is 29½ ounces, for example. Sizes are closely correlated to weights. The 111B has a base of about seven inches square and stands four inches high. The Svea is three-and-three-quarter inches in diameter and five inches high.

What do you get in return for carrying a bigger stove? Stability, for one thing. The heavier the stove, the bigger the base and lower center of gravity it probably has; thus it is less apt to topple over with a pot on it.

This doesn't always apply, however; a stove's design contributes to its stability. For example, the light MSR has a unique "outrigger" in the form of a fuel bottle. It lies on its side and is connected to the stove's burner by a stiff metal tube, about five inches long. The bottle serves as a fuel chamber, the stove having none. In spite of the three-and-a-half inch diameter of the burner itself, the entire assembly spreads out to almost a foot across. This design makes the MSR extremely stable.

Another design feature of the stove also stands out. It provides copious fuel without the penalty of added weight. Either a pint or quart bottle hooks up, through the metal tube to the burner, as the fuel chamber. Almost all campers carry a reserve fuel bottle anyhow, in addition to a stove.

You usually get greater fuel capacity with a larger stove. The Optimus 111B holds a pint, as does the 2½ pound Phoebus 625. Again, design is important. You can put six ounces into the small Svea's chamber, but the Optimus 8R, weighing twenty-three ounces, holds less than four ounces. On a Bikecentennial tour I led, I found that the latter had to be filled frequently, sometimes awkwardly in the midst of making a meal. For a group, which needs a lot of hot water for beverages and dishwashing, look for more fuel in the tank and a longer burn time.

A larger fuel tank doesn't necessarily mean proportionately longer burning, though. For example, the Coleman Backpacker holds ten ounces compared to the MSR's fifteen ounces (in a pint fuel bottle). The Coleman burns for seventy-five minutes at full speed and the MSR one hundred minutes, roughly comparable times for the amount of fuel. But at a fast simmer, Coleman's burning time increases to three and a half hours, and the MSR to only one hundred and thirty minutes. At still a lower simmer, a Coleman runs even longer. MSR's stove won't burn evenly at such a low flame and you can't get a low simmer from it. The difference between the two stoves in low-burning times is this ability to control a simmer; more about this point later.

Larger white gas stoves, and those using kerosene too, usually work better in cold weather. Smaller ones cool faster, with a subsequent loss of pressure. You can insulate any stove from very cold ground with a piece of three-eighth inch ensolite, and it will help slow the loss of pressure. Cut a piece about the diameter of the stove base and pack it with the stove.

Cold weather operation may not be as important a consideration in road travel as in mountain climbing, but you do get cool evenings and mornings even in summer. You might do well to use an aluminum-covered windscreen around your stove and pot, as will be described shortly.

Everything else being equal, you're probably better off to carry two small stoves for a group trip than the equivalent weight in one large one. The two burners would give you more flexibility. If one broke down for some reason, the other would still serve. You'd also be able to cook two dishes simultaneously, shortening cooking time and enlarging the scope of your menus.

The trouble is that all things aren't equal. Larger stoves are less temperamental; small ones tend to be hard starters and erratic. But those very qualities seem to challenge their owners. Bruce Ohlson of Sacramento tells, with relish, of his tactics in taming his Svea. Sandy Clark of Rock Hill, South Carolina, and Ray Phelps of Columbia, Maryland also commented, with some satisfaction, on having to learn that stove's peculiarities. And of course Colin Fletcher has almost sanctified the rituals of its operation in his book, *The Complete Walker.* Some people are just born masochists, it seems.

Built-in features are convenient, but you can pump up a stove, clean it, and shield it against wind with accessories. Optimus sells an accessory pump that fits all its stoves, for example. Three cleaning needles cost under a dollar and can be used with any stove; they last for years.

Most windscreens that are part of the stove's design are useless or only partially effective; you can make a better screen yourself. Bender Hash made one of aluminum foil taped on cardboard for his stove. Bruce Ohlson fashioned a windscreen out of one-eighth inch plywood. He cut three pieces, eight by eight inches each, and used duct tape for hinges. His flexible three-sided screen adapts to any size stove and allows the use of larger pans. It's surprising that some manufacturer hasn't made one like it.

Such a windscreen can also help reflect heat back to the pot and conserve its heat in cold weather, in the way that the MSR stove kit does. A safety precaution here, though: the MSR's fuel is kept outside of the screen and stays cool. Your screen may reflect too much heat onto the tank and be dangerous. Feel the tank to check that it doesn't get too warm.

Maintenance of stoves and the availability of spare parts are important considerations. Most can be cleaned easily, but some may require special tools and replacement parts. Spare parts, even built-in cleaning needles, were difficult to get for my Phoebus 625. It's best not to buy a stove without getting spares at the same time. Also examine the maintenance booklet, if available.

In spite of the caution of the manufacturers against it, some stoves can be used with unleaded gas. I've used a number of them that way without any real harm and with just a bit of inconvenience. Other backpack stove users told me of their similar experience, and RV campers said they've used Coleman's own multi-burner stoves with no-lead gas. I've also heard from two people who spoke to fuel engineers. The latter told them that the use of unleaded gas does no harm, except in catalytic burners. I believe Mr. Coleman may have the stove industry brainwashed in the belief that only the purest fuels can be used.

I used unleaded in my Phoebus 625 for nine months on the United States trip. I've also filled the Optimus 8R and the Svea with it, although for shorter tours. The practice cost me a few cleaning needles and necessitated a general cleaning of jets and orifices about once a month. But I noted no drop in efficiency in any of those stoves. I did get a lot of soot collected on pots and the stove, but it was due mostly to a problem with simmering, a subject I'll discuss shortly. You can avoid some of this pot blackening by placing the lid of a can between the pot and fire. The lid also helps distribute heat along the bottom.

Only one manufacturer claims its stove can be used with either regular or no-lead pump gas, and that only cautiously. Mountain Safety Research states that its multi-fuel model MSR-GK (white gas, kerosene, Stoddard solvent, No. 1 stove oil, No. 1 diesel, JP-4, and even alcohol) can burn car gas "in an emergency—when the recommended fuels are not available." MSR suggests that the jet opening be poked with a cleaning wire with each use and that the jet, surge damper, and fuel cable be taken out and cleaned after about two pints, if performance suffers. My experience with the stove confirms automotive fuel use; I don't sense any loss of power with that fiery workhorse. George Pohl, a bicyclist from Philadelphia, swears by it, and other bikers tell me how powerful it is.

In fact, the only real problem with gas stoves—almost all of them in my estimation—is not power at all. Just the opposite: most are too efficient at the high end. They insist on literally roaring their fire out of the jet—what MSR calls its "turbulent flame"—and you're hard put to tone them down. You try for gentleness and you get a blowtorch; food sticks and water steams away.

Just like automotive companies in their horsepower races of a few years ago, stove makers are today in a fuel efficiency race. Most are convinced that the first duty of a stove is to melt snow into water and to produce gallons of boiling water. Instead of concentrating on the reduction of boiling time, a manufacturer would do better to keep efficiency at what it is now and improve simmering control instead. I would consider this a significant design improvement, suited to a real need of a large group of campers.

I have direct experience with seven white gas stoves: Coleman's Backpacker, Phoebus' 625 and the 725, the MSR-GK, Optimus' 99 and the 8R and the Svea 123. Only the first two have satisfactory simmer control. Coleman's is the most effective, with separate controls for gas regulation and for on-off. You can bottom out at the lowest position of the regular control without the flame going out or wavering; a definite plus.

In all other stoves I know of, one control handles both the gas flow and the off position, off being another small turn beyond the slowest gas flow. This control is usually a hair trigger. When you turn the flame too low, it either goes out or changes from a blue flame to an inefficient candlelight. The yellow flame can maintain a simmer, but it soon clogs internal passages and the jet.

The Phoebus can also maintain a simmer, although less easily than the Coleman. It has a single-control handle—large and with a fairly good sweep for fine adjustment—but the wheel has to be manipulated carefully to find the appropriate setting. The tank pressure must also be lowered, else the flame gets too high. The Phoebus stove has never gone out in a wind when I used it, although the flame would blow sideways in a strong breeze.

The Phoebus 725 holds ten ounces of fuel and weighs one-and-a-half pounds. Most of its parts are interchangeable with the 625, and it has the stability and ruggedness of its bigger brother. Jon Gross, a tour leader for Vermont Bicycle Touring, burns unleaded gas in the 725 with no problems. He wrote that it takes just minutes to boil water when cooking corn for his group of twenty-five or more. Jon likes that stove's reliability and efficiency, but he does complain that its low flame burns "dirty."

It's interesting to note that stoves using less efficient fuels, such as alcohol or butane, have better simmering controls than white gas models. You can turn them down to almost out, and the flame still burns clean and steady. But alcohol and butane stoves lose out on the high end of the flame. Therein lies a dilemma for the user. He must choose between these two extremes of performance.

One solution is to buy one of each type stove for those times when you use two: use white gas for boiling and a butane for simmering. If you carry only one stove you must do something else, though. The manufacturer's suggestions for simmering are usually scant. Understandably, they concentrate very little on the control valve. They seem to recognize that this is largely a misnomer; the control is crude. Manufacturers do focus more on reducing pressure in the tank, on removing the lid from the pot, or the windscreen from around the stove.

Releasing pressure, and then repumping the stove for a stroke or two, as manufacturers suggest, is awkward. At worst, you must set the pot aside, see to the pressure change and then hope the dish hasn't lost its heat in the interim. At best, it disturbs your timing. On some stoves with a pump, like the Phoebus, releasing pressure is fairly easy. You just open the fuel tank cover slightly, to release the pressure, and then pump a stroke or two. With others that have tanks that heat up a lot, it might be impossible since high pressure is continually maintained.

If you remove the windscreen and the wind blows, you may boil one minute and not have enough, or any, flame the next. I've had the flame on small stoves blow sideways. At these times the whole cooking operation had to be transferred to the lee of a building. In the absence of shelter, three of us would line up in front of the stove, in close order like wooden soldiers, to block the wind. As for taking the lid off the pot to reduce the effect of heat, how would you then build up steam for cooking rice? No, you need more reliable ways to lower heat output.

There are all kinds of expedients. One uses an asbestos simmering pad; it dampens the heat and dissipates it slightly. The heat is at least spread evenly throughout the pot's bottom. Sears sells a circular pad just under nine inches in diameter, about a half pound. Combined with the lowest setting of the control valve, this pad may give you a satisfactory simmer—if you're using a large pot containing a lot of food, and if the tank pressure is moderately low.

Be careful of using the pad or a wide pan on some stoves. They can reflect heat back onto the fuel tank and overheat, with the danger of blowing out the safety valve. You'll have a neat Roman candle then, and perhaps some singed hair. Some manufacturers warn you against this danger, others don't. With MSR's stove, there is no such problem; the tank is well away from the burner.

Another method involves raising the pot away from the flame. The pan support wires can be bent upwards on some stoves, positioning the stove higher away from the flame. The effect is not all that profound, but it does help with stoves that don't burn too hot to start with. The time needed to reach a boil would be increases somewhat, unless you bend the wires back down again. You couldn't do that too many times; the wires would soon snap off.

With just a little bother, a double boiler can be concocted to reduce heat. Suspend the smaller of two nesting pots on stones or any small platform inside the larger pot; fill the larger one partially with water. The consequent removal of the smaller pot from the direct flame takes away enough heat to control a simmer.

All these measures work, to a degree, but the best solution would be for the stove maker to design a sensitive control system, one which would approximate what you can get on a kitchen stove. A good system may already exist, but I've not seen it yet.

Mind you, I'm not suggesting a return to campfire cooking. The improvement of the stove upon the open fire in controlling heat output is substantial. The twist of a stove's control valve, however jerky, is a quantum leap above the adjustment of the pot's position over hot coals.

All factors considered, my personal preferences in stoves are multiple, each dependent on the use intended. For lengthy travel in America I like a large stove, using white gas. My kind of cooking calls for a slow simmer. I need a long burning time, more than two hours without refilling, not only for cooking but to heat water for beverages and washing. I also want a fuel that  is reasonably cheap and readily available.

I don't know of any small stove, no matter the fuel, that could give me this combination of features. They are all light and efficient, great for backpackers who boil freeze-dried packets and melt snow, but they don't do for me.

Two large stoves that do possess these features are the Phoebus 625 and the Coleman Backpacker. The choice between them would rest on additional factors. The Backpacker has the edge in simmering ability, and it needs no preheating except in cold weather.

Coleman has recently introduced a new, lighter version of its stove, the model 400 (the older one is 576). Four ounces of weight has been trimmed and its packed height was reduced about a quarter inch. Fold-out legs improve its stability; they effectively extend its base diameter to almost six and a half inches, a gain of two and a half inches. Otherwise, its operating characteristics are the same.

Arguing for the Phoebus, I know from long personal experience that I can use pump gas with it, although at some inconvenience in the form of soot and additional maintenance. The ability to use pump gas is an important advantage where white gas is inconvenient to carry or hard to get. I hesitate to try no-lead with the Coleman, for fear that it would clog and be too difficult to maintain in the field.

Overseas, in Asia and other backwaters, I'd bring the MSR-GK. It would enable me to use any liquid fuel that is locally available, my prevailing criterion in strange lands. I'd also feel completely confident that with a few spares I could maintain this stove by myself, no matter what might happen. Its maintenance manual is probably the best available, and the procedures described in it almost foolproof. If that stove could only simmer well—important to me—it would be the only one I'd use.

For yet another kind of need, a trip of a few days, I'd take along the Optimus Mousetrap and settle for making simple meals. One full cartridge would last a long weekend. I'd also carry this lightweight stove as a useful back-up with a group, to shorten meal making with the second burner and to act as an emergency reserve. Unfortunately, the LP cartridges used in this stove are not available outside of the United States. Overseas, I'd bring one of the butane stoves which use the internationally available Camping Gaz 200 cartridges.

If you were to follow my advice, you'd have to invest in a few stoves. But this is justified only if you camp in a variety of situations as I do. Should your camping needs be of only one kind, on the other hand, choose the stove to fit that use. Your investment in a few stoves, prorated over their lives for a number of years, would be very modest in any case, and your cooking potential would be vastly improved.

# Let's Get Organized

A cook is like the captain of a ship—resolute in decision and in absolute command. No matter what the pecking order is on the road, once in the campground he's in charge. The others may get tired and cross, tempers can rise and the organization may waver, but the cook keeps a cool head and maintains the course: he has no time for weakness or hysterics.

The cook receives priority in group services and enjoys the privilege of rank. He picks the camping site, gets help from the group in setting it up, and chooses the menu.

He's exempt from menial tasks such as fetching water, washing and chopping vegetables, and cleaning up. There's an assistant—some will call him a "sous-chef," others a lackey—to take care of those chores and to supply him with needed ingredients. That assistant also washes everyone's dishes. For the cook, it's enough to concentrate on the preparation of the meal.

During my long trips, we designated the cook for a stable length of time, a few days or a week. After that tour of duty, the assistant graduated to the cook's job for the next period. He now acquired a new assistant from the group. We always sandwiched the less experienced people between more skillful ones. This system insured continuity and helped train those who had little cooking know-how.

Ours was pretty much a loose ship; the cook was more in command of a rowboat than a dreadnought. He had an oarsman and occasional volunteers, who helped him when time was crucial or when more hands were needed, but the others were basically passengers rather than crew. They enjoyed freedom from cooking responsibilities until their turn would come at the helm.

The cook's duties should start with picking a campground. There's often a wide choice in a tourist area, or where private and public camps compete for customers. You're more likely to be less crowded in a campground that lacks the elaborate conveniences that trailerites seek. On a bike, or even in a car, you don't need a level concrete ramp, electric and water hookups, a children's play area, and a holding-tank disposal. You won't be likely to enjoy a swim in a pool, since you usually arrive late in the day and leave early in the morning. You pay for all those features in the higher price of a KOA or other deluxe camps. Why support the luxuries of the RV crowd?

For ultimate economy, camp in the woods, at a park, a farmer's field (ask permission if you can find the owner, often difficult), or at a rest stop on the highway. Water can usually be carted into these places, if it's not there already. Even when it is expressly forbidden to camp at a rest stop, police don't enforce the restriction with a bicyclist if they can see that you're not able to ride in the dark to the next organized campground. I've never had trouble this way, either alone or in a group. Maybe the prospect of carting riders with pack-laden bikes was too much for the rural patrol car.

When there is no water, you might be tempted to use a stream or lake as a source of cooking water. I fight it, personally. Even when you boil such water you're taking a chance. It may contain minerals and chemicals that boiling wouldn't help eliminate. There are very few places in the world where water is really pure. I've read that Lake Baikal in Siberia is completely polluted, and most American waters are in the same shape.

The safe sources are the melting snow runoff in mountain areas that have no factories or large settlements. These are found in scattered places in the American west, as well as elsewhere in the world. In Turkey the government has installed hundreds of taps along mountain roads. Water flows from those in a continual runoff, and townspeople make special trips to collect water. I thought it the freshest I've ever tasted.

Economy aside, it's sometimes a pleasant change to enjoy new company in a campground's community hall, to do your laundry, and to be able to buy some additional food items or a nighttime snack from the camp store. Those comforts are usually absent in the small private campground and almost always missing in state or national parks.

Try to arrive in camp a couple of hours before dark—it's more pleasant to see what you're eating. At the start of our Edge trip, before we became organized, we often ate in the dark; we never knew how many insects we ingested, but it must have been many. The cooks will make fewer mistakes and the group will be more relaxed when there's no pressure of impending darkness.

Some attention should be paid to choosing a desirable site. First there may not be many options; the camp may be crowded or the sites may all be equal in quality. But if there is a choice, you should pick a spot not too far from the bathrooms and certainly not far from water. In a few overseas camps in Poland and Mexico, as well as a place or two in the United States, I was cautioned not to camp near the fence if I planned to go somewhere and leave my things unguarded. Because it was more remote from the office, the edge of the camp was said to be more accessible to youngsters who'd jump in and steal loose objects.

When a campsite adjoining yours has disadvantages, e.g., is rocky or on a slope, it's not apt to be occupied later by other campers. It's a good one to be next to. You can carry over its table to your site and have the use of two, one for cooking and the other for group social use. With a large group of riders, you may have to pay for two campsites anyhow. Four tents or persons are usually the most allowed at one site.

If the group is tired and touchy from the day's riding, it's best to stay shy of neighbors with children. The little darlings may be charming otherwise, but they can try the patience of harassed cooks. On the other hand, children may prove to be a welcome change from the forced company of your own group. And they are often the keys to the hearts of their parents, those good people who might contribute some goodies to your supper table and ply you with interesting talk and cold beer later that evening.

The cooks should get right to the job at hand: no tent-erecting, coffee-sipping, or dawdling. With only time out to wash hands—showers can be taken later—they set up the kitchen.

What kitchen? Why, the kitchen on the redwood table if you have one, or on a stone grill's surface, tree stump, or any territory that is staked out by the cook. That turf should be inviolable during meal preparation time. The group can use it later to eat on, but it should be off limits in the meantime. Let the gossip, unloading of personal gear, and the horseplay go on somewhere else. Leave the cooks' area to them.

At mealtimes, especially in the first few days of a tour when all hands are cooperative beyond belief, hungry bikers are eager to help with the cooking. The cook should staunchly resist these offers, except to allow helpers to fetch water or move tables. Volunteer help is often more a hindrance. It gives license to taste, relate distracting stories, to criticize, and kibitz—all detrimental to the business at hand. Simply ask your comrades to unload the cooking gear that they may be carrying onto the table and go away.

Start the fire first thing, even before washing up. The stove is invariably black with carbon and you'd need to wash again anyhow. Fill the stove with fuel before each session. It's frustrating to run out in the middle of cooking rice or pasta. Put water on at once for tea, cocoa, or coffee. It will abate some of the clamor of the group for instant, McDonald's-like satisfaction.

Cut open a large shopping bag or two and spread the paper on your work space to keep the operation clean. We always asked for extra bags when we shopped, and used them to mix salads (minus the dressing), to store prepared dishes that had to be held until later, and as cutting surfaces.

Decide the sequence of cooking steps to avoid conflict or confusion. Review the recipe by reading it through. As you do, pull out the spices and other ingredients that you'll need. Measure them out on pieces of paper, dry ones first and wet afterwards to save washing and drying the spoon and cup in between. Put away what you're through with and won't use later.

For safety's sake, pans should be set well away from the edges of the table. Always keep in mind Murphy's Law to avoid accidents. I remember vividly an occasion when I hit a pot of stroganoff with my elbow. It flipped neatly upside down onto the seat of the picnic table. We had nothing else with us to eat that evening and were forced to scoop up the top half of that mess. Watch out when you pour boiling water into coffee cups, especially when it's getting dark and hard to see. I was once burned by such a spill, which fell through the slits of the planked table onto my lap.

What about when it rains? At best, it's a nuisance. With luck, you might have the use of the campground's community hall (where you may well sleep afterwards). At worst it's hell, with water flowing into ingredients and chilling the food.

Even when rain is not imminent, it's a good precaution to be within a short run of a community hall or a sheltered picnic area. Many times we were surprised by a sudden rainstorm and ran for the dry spot, with one carrying the burning stove, another the pot, and the rest of the group lugging sundry items. The authorities never forbade it, once it began to rain, even when such a spot was off-limits for cooking purposes.

If at all possible find shelter of some kind when on the road, even if you have to ride in the downpour a few extra miles. You might be able to use an abandoned building, a gazebo in a town square, a bus stop shelter, or the overhang of a small store. Such a store's owner may be more apt to honor your request to cook supper outside of his store if you buy your groceries from him. He'd be a source of water too.

When caught in the open, all riders should immediately set up their tents' flysheets. Forget the tents themselves for the moment. Overlap these flysheets as much as possible to create a widespread shelter—a supertent. If you are among some trees with convenient, low-hanging branches, one or more of the flies can be stretched overhead.

Although some rain may still get through overhead or from the side, the enforced togetherness is both efficient of space and heartening psychologically. Rain is most devastating when it forces each camper to suffer in solitude, without commiseration with others.

More important for the cooking effort, the shelter affords more room for meal preparation, dining, and cleaning up. You may even use water run-off to satisfy your water needs.

Don't cook in a tent; the fumes may overcome you. Oxygen is rapidly consumed by the flame even in the best ventilated tents, and you won't know what hit you, or you could burn holes in the tent itself.

But if the rain gets too oppressive, you might toss in the towel and head for the nearest restaurant for a feast. The group can vote on it, of course, but I've never known wet and chilled travelers who turned it down. At such a time, there's nothing for the soul like being warm and indoors.

# Down to Basics

My son Stephen and his new bride Janet were both just beginning to enjoy the pleasures of cooking. They complained: "It was a great recipe you gave us, and easy to make, but it took forever to chop everything."

That's a more common stumbling block than most cookbooks acknowledge. They take it for granted that everyone knows how to cut, measure, get organized, and follow directions. But beginners usually spend more time cutting ingredients, piece by laborious piece, than in the actual cooking. And they interrupt the process frequently to re-read recipes because they don't understand exactly what's to be done.

I keep before me the model of my good friend, Clarke Bachman, when I think of the typical beginner. As a conversationalist, a savant on matters artistic and civilized, and as a sensitive human being, he was superior. As a cook he was helpless.

Clarke tried my patience often with his culinary clumsiness. Yet, he learned. He seemed the least likely to succeed at first. I believe he now has the confidence to cook for himself because of his experience on our Edge trip. I try to anticipate beginners' problems by recalling some of Clarke's.

Before a child can run, it must first learn to take steps; before one can cook confidently, he or she must acquire some basic skills. Here are a few that need more explanation and practice than just a brief reading of definitions:

42

*Chopping* and *dicing*. Not that at all, unless you mean the lightning rat-tat-tat that Oriental cooks use to cut vegetables with those huge knife-cleavers of theirs. You had better not try that for awhile, not until you have more experience with a sharp knife and not unless you want an end of your finger to be included in the dish.

Chopping is really cutting or slicing, usually vegetables but often fruit, into pieces about three-eighths of an inch or less, square or cubed. It is best done systematically.

Take an onion, for example. Peel it, then cut the onion in half from stem to root. Keep the root intact to help hold the layers together. Lay the half down on the cutting surface, on its flat side and with the root opposite to you. Now make a series of parallel slices, still along the stem-root axis, all the way down but just short of the root. Use a sharp knife and cut three-eighths of an inch apart.

You now have a grid of columns from stem to root. Hold it all together; if you let go, the onion may open into a wondrous flower—esthetically a joy but difficult to cut further.

Turn the onion ninety degrees, so that the root end is now toward your left side. Slice at right angles to the previous cuts, again 3/8 inch apart. Hundreds of tiny cubes will be released, like dandelion seeds scattering in a breeze. When you're almost done you'll find it difficult to hold. Go as far as you can, until there's a bit of stub left. Throw it away (or chop it up if you're frugal) and then chop the other half.

The same technique, making some modifications for different shapes, is used for celery (lay a number of stalks on top of each other, slice lengthwise, then across) and other vegetables and fruit.

To *chop finely* is to make closer slices, about a quarter-inch or less if you can manage it. To *mince* is to go even finer and is more difficult. Chop finely first, then make a final series of cuts by holding the tip of a knife steady with a fingertip, while making rapid chopping motions at the handle end around an arc. Leafy things like parsley or fresh herbs can be minced with scissors. Happily, mincing is called for only occasionally.

*Measuring* is sometimes critical, sometimes not. Measure accurately as a habit, unless it's a matter of taste on items like sugar and spice. It won't do any harm and it can help.

The common technique for using measuring spoons is to fill them and then level off any excess with a knife or other straight edge. Don't try to measure butter or margarine with a cup or measuring spoon. Use sticks of butter and cut them proportionately—one stick equals eight tablespoons.

Measuring flour or other pulverized ingredients often calls for *sifting*. A sifter introduces air into the ingredients and causes expansion. It also makes mixing with other ingredients more thorough. The technique is important in baking and it does affect measuring, since it changes the volume of the material.

Since we do no baking in these pages, it doesn't matter to us in that respect. Our recipes use flour in quick breads, as a thickener and for coating meats. The amount in these recipes is flexible. In quick breads and pancakes, expanding air does have a function—lumpy flour and sugar can make flat pancakes. For this reason, it's a good practice to "quasi-sift" by lifting and tossing the dry ingredients while combining them.

*Beating* an egg or a batter is done with a whisk, fork, or spoon. Use a large enough vessel so that the contents won't spill out. Rotate the whisk in an over-and-under motion through the material, in an oval direction.

When beating egg whites or cream to make them *stiff*, you'll need to *whip* them very rapidly. Stiff means that they set up in "peaks." You'll need a whisk for this operation, not a fork. Even so, it will take some time to stiffen them. But if egg whites are not completely set up after five to ten minutes of hard work, use them as is. Whipped cream should set up easier.

*Folding* the stiffened whites into yolks or batter is like beating, except in very slow motion so as not to lose the texture of the beaten whites. The purpose is to lighten the omelet or pancake with all the air you've incorporated into the whites.

Before any whipping or folding of whites, you *separate* the whites from the yolks, of course. Crack the egg through and split the two halves, but don't break them apart yet. Let most of the white fall out into your collecting dish. Then pass the yolk back and forth a few times from one half to the other, letting more white fall out. Use your finger tip to push out the bit of white that always seems to cling to the shell.

If a yolk breaks and some of it mixes with the white, forget it. You'll never get it to stiffen. For this reason it's a good idea to use two dishes when separating a number of eggs. Do one at a time in the first dish and transfer the white to the other. If you have a mishap only one egg will be affected. Don't throw it out; add it to the yolks.

When I first started cooking I took *timing* very seriously; so much so that I used to wait until the second hand came to twelve before beginning. Since then, I've stopped wearing a watch at all. This was more a consequence of my adopting a new, unhurried lifestyle on a bicycle than a lackadaisical attitude towards time. I still carry a watch on bike trips, but it comes out of the pannier only at cooking time.

I've learned that timing isn't sacrosanct. It is so affected by several variables that two meals, cooked on different days but following the same recipe, may not be done to the same degree even though their times are identical. The meats or vegetables may differ in tenderness, for example, or another stove-pan combination may distribute the heat differently through the contents.

The stove's contribution to this timing is minimal. Its efficiency is a measure of the heat it generates for a given amount of fuel, not how fast it will cook your meal. True, one stove may take a few minutes less to bring your stew to an initial boil than another. But beyond that point, *simmering* is what counts. Even an inefficient stove can hold that simmer; it's on a par with any other where timing is concerned.

The diameter of a stove's burner does have an appreciable effect on the cooking process: the wider the flame, the more even the heat distribution and the shorter the cooking time. Larger camping stoves have somewhat broader burners (about two and a quarter inches for the Phoebus 625 and Coleman's Backpacker, for example) than smaller ones (one and three-quarter inches for Optimus 99 and 731 models). For group cooking with big pots, this would be an additional reason to use a large stove. But all camping stoves are vastly inferior to the kitchen range which has burners with minimum diameters of three inches.

The pot makes the greatest contribution to timing. A thin-walled container loses heat fast, and cooking tends to be uneven and prolonged. In cold weather its contents may be simmering at the bottom but cold to the touch at the surface. A large pot is harder to heat evenly than a small one, given a small burner—twelve inches of pot bottom distributes heat less evenly than does seven inches, unless it's copper-clad or extra thick to make distribution even. (See "The Logistics of the Bike-Kitchen" for further discussion of pot characteristics.)

Still, without some foundation there would be chaos. Use the times given in individual recipes as a guide. Start timing a simmer from the point at which the contents of the pot begin to boil, or just before. Then turn the heat down, short of any breaking bubbles or occasional ones at the surface.

After cooking a few meals with your stove-pan combination, you may note that it consistently takes you more or less time than I've indicated. Adjust accordingly. You shouldn't be too far off, however. The times given are based on an average of my experience with various camping equipment, not on the kitchen range.

In addition to timing, *test* as you go along. Jab the meat or potatoes with a fork when time is almost up. If the fork goes in easily, they're done. Taste vegetables and pasta for tenderness, to your liking. There's nothing sacred in the clock's hands.

When *browning* or *sauteeing*, use a visual check. Both of these techniques use a small amount of fat after preheating the pan well. Browning, sometimes referred to as *searing*, is accomplished by cooking for a short time over a hot flame. Meat will lose its raw look, although it may not actually turn brown, and onions will turn yellow to yellow-brown. The main intent of browning is to seal in meat juices behind a toughened "skin," before cooking further, but it also imparts a chewier surface which many find pleasant. I do.

To *saute* is to fry over a medium flame for a somewhat longer time. Onions and mushrooms, and other sensitively textured vegetables, are commonly sauteed. Onions and celery lose their opaque look and may yellow slightly when done.

*Spices* always lend excitement—spice things up, as the saying goes. They should not be overused, lest the excitement turns to frenzy and finally to satiation. The United States and England seem to be the only countries that avoid the wide use of spices. The farther east one goes in the world, the more condiments one finds in food.

Spices release their flavor best when heated or when leafy or solid pieces are shredded between the fingers before adding. The only exception to this would be a bayleaf, which you'd want to retrieve from the dish after its use in cooking.

Spices should be kept cool and airless; whole leaves, stems, and seeds keep better than powders. But these forms need more space in containers, awkward for our purposes, and I carry mostly ground versions for this reason. Since I use them up soon enough, spoilage never bothers me.

# Let's Practice

If you can make a decent omelet or fluffy rice on a one-burner stove you've got it half licked. These simple accomplishments mean you've attained control—tamed the fire, measured correctly, and knew when to stop the process.

Small potatoes, say you experienced cooks? For someone who had never before prepared anything more elaborate than a TV dinner, as was the case with Clarke Bachman, those are major steps that lead to more complicated dishes.

Practicing under the eyes of a more experienced cook, a mother or a friend, is best. The novice is shown directly those mysterious points at which eggs are "firmed up" or rice has "absorbed all the water it can." Words are only approximations.

In the absence of that kind of direct guidance, a few sessions in your own home before you take your tour are next best. Make those practice meals on your one-burner; the gas range in your home is a poor place on which to train for on-tour cooking. Use only those ingredients and the utensils you plan to take along. With these few pots and aids, you can learn the game of musical chairs you'll need to play with limited gear on the road. And practice with your companion-to-be, if possible. This would heighten the realism and give you both a chance to try out a team effort.

The two recipes I suggest for practice aren't difficult, but they do include techniques basic to all cooking. I offer them with a running commentary to give a sense of sequence. The first, for chicken curry, takes a fairly long time to prepare, mostly because of the number of ingredients that must be made ready. (See appendix for the abbreviations used.)

**Chicken Curry**

| | |
|---|---|
| 2 chicken breasts, boned | 1/2 lb. sweet potato, cubed 1" |
| 3 stalks celery, chopped | 2 hardboiled eggs (optional) |
| 2 onions, chopped | 2 bananas (optional) |
| 1 clove garlic, minced | 2 med. apples, cubed 3/4" |
| 3 T vegetable oil | handful of raisins |
| 1 1/2 c. chicken bouillon | 1/4 c. flour |
| 1 c. tomato juice | 1/4 c. water |
| 1 1/2 T curry powder | shredded coconut (optional) |
| 1 t. salt | peanuts |

Cut the chicken into bite sized pieces. It's easier to do this with chicken that comes boned than to cut it off the bone yourself. Saute the chicken in oil, over a medium flame, along with the celery, onion, and garlic. (Your assistant chopped those–see chapter 5 for chopping techniques.) You can saute right in the 4 quart pot you'll use for the entire dish; no need for a frying pan. Cook until the onion starts looking transparent, about five minutes. Add the bouillon. (You can buy this in cans or make it yourself. Just add dry cubes of bouillon, cut into smaller pieces, toss into hot water and dissolve. Use a couple of them in this recipe; usually you use one per cup.) Mix in the tomato, curry, salt, and potato. Bring to a boil and immediately lower the flame so that the liquid simmers. Here's where a heat suppressor, or asbestos pad, comes in handy if your stove lacks a low control. Simmer covered for about twenty minutes, or until a fork can just penetrate the meat easily. Test it first after fifteen minutes. While the pot is cooking away, make rice if you have another stove. If not, prepare all the ingredients for six cups of cooked rice (see the basic rice recipe in part 2 of this book). You'll need a second pot for rice, of course. If you have only one pot, the rice can be made first and set aside in someone's mess kit. Place the container of rice in a paper bag and cover with a sleeping bag to keep it warm until the rest of the meal is ready. The pot can then be used for the curry. Once the chicken mixture is ready, add chopped up eggs, sliced bananas, apples, and raisins. Apples need not be peeled. Mix flour in the water. It'll dissolve easily in cold water; don't use hot. Add this to the pot and simmer five minutes longer. The flour will thicken your curry by this time.

You're done! Serve the rice, and spoon or pour the curry mixture over it. Each person can sprinkle with peanuts and coconut to taste. This recipe will fill the hungry stomachs of about four bicyclists. For just one additional biker, you can get away by simply making more rice or eating bread with the meal. The curry will stretch.

Of course, the directions you usually get in a cookbook are abbreviated. They are terse and assume basic cooking knowledge. The typical recipe might look like this:

**Mexican Cumin**

| | |
|---|---|
| 1/2 lb. each, ground beef and pork | 1 1/2 lbs. canned tomatoes |
| 2 onions, chopped | 1 t. salt |
| 1 green pepper, chopped | 1 1/2 T chili powder |
| 1/2 c. water | 1/4 t. cumin powder |
| 2 c. plain yogurt | 1/2 lb. thin spaghetti |

Brown meat, onion, and pepper; drain. Break meat into pieces. Cook pork first for twenty minutes, covered, and drain before browning. Add rest, one at a time, stirring. Add spaghetti, broken up, when liquid is boiling and continue a fast simmer for ten minutes, or until pasta is tender to the taste. Stir frequently.

Recipes like this one, in which rice or noodles are cooked at once with the rest of the dish, are tricky. They take a lot of continuous stirring when using thin pots. They'll stick to the bottom otherwise, and the food will get burned.

You may have to substitute or change the amount of ingredients sometimes. In the above recipe, for example, a large noodle may be all the pasta that's available in the store. Or buttermilk may have to do for yogurt. You may have to adjust the cooking time for the pasta. The package will tell how long to cook. Watch the density of the mixture too. If it starts getting thick, for whatever reason, add water or more yogurt.

It may be that your group would prefer more or less meat in

relation to filler. You might also want to change the amount of spice, depending on others' tastes. During hot weather or periods of heavy exertion, salt may have to be increased. Try the basic recipe first; it's not a rigid formula, but a starting point.

Although both these recipes could be called one-pot meals, you'll note that for the chicken curry this is really a misnomer. Everything ended up in one pot, but other containers were needed to hold ingredients and to cook the rice. It was possible, in other words, to cook the meal simultaneously over two stoves and speed things. The value of group sharing of pots and having more than one stove is evident here. Not only can you save time overall, but water can be heated for other purposes.

If you have only one stove, you need not wait idly for each step to be completed to go on to the next. As noted in the chicken recipe, preparatory steps can be taken for the other operations. A stove's operation can be interrupted to start the cooking of another part of the meal, too. For example, with a meat and potatoes meal, you could start the meat cooking and bring it to about five minutes from done. Then set that pan aside and cook the potatoes. The meat will get cold, but it doesn't matter. When the potatoes are done, put the meat back on. Mash the potatoes while the meat reheats. By this shifting, the meal comes out with all dishes hot.

# Cleaning Up the Mess

Stomach problems usually acquire exotic, foreign names: Montezuma's revenge, Delhi belly, the Turkey trot. Blame is attributed to an outside evil, or an intruding microbe floating in the air from some unknown source. But the fault is often our own sanitation, or lack of it; the enemy is us. Good clean-up habits prevent diarrhea.

Removing food completely from eating utensils is the most important aspect of hygiene during a trip. You may not take a bath for weeks or never brush your teeth; it will make you smelly and uncomfortable, but you won't get sick and won't necessarily contaminate someone else. Food traces left to spoil on a cooking pot, on the other hand, will affect everyone.

Hot water is our salvation. You're in luck if you're in a campground that has it. Although most camps forbid diswashing in the sinks, because deposits of grease can clog pipes, there's nothing wrong with drawing hot sink water and washing your dishes outside in some designated spot.

Even with hot water available, you'll still have to boil it, since most tap water is not hot enough to sanitize in the last, scalding rinse. For this reason, as well as to keep a constant source of tea or coffee, it's best not to turn off the stove and to keep water heating when nothing else is cooking.

Before washing your eating equipment, encourage everyone to remove all the food from plates with bread—wasting food is a sin, my mother used to say—and use crumpled bags, toilet paper, or even leaves or pine needles to wipe off the last bit. In areas with sand or loose dirt, utensils can be thrust into the ground to loosen residue and then brushed off. Handfuls of earth can also be rubbed around pots and pans, but not those with non-stick surfaces. A preliminary "cleaning" of this kind makes further washing easier. Rinsing with cold water helps too.

Don't try to wash soot off the bottom of pots. There's no need to coat them with soap beforehand either. Simply wipe the soot with wads of paper. You can wash afterwards or let it go as long as the soot doesn't rub off on your hands or inside your panniers.

Practice washing two separate times, even when plenty of water is available. The two washes are more efficient than the equivalent effort in one. The first will invariably still leave the water a bit greasy. The second wash will insure cleanliness.

Use a biodegradable soap like Ivory Snow. It's ecologically right and it doubles for clothes washing. However, the small packages sold in laundromats are a poor buy. Get a box, do a big laundry, and keep what's left over in a double layer of strong plastic bags. It will last several weeks.

A plastic scrubber is better than a sponge or a steel wool pad. A sponge retains germs more efficiently than plastic bristles; the objection to steel wool is clear if you have Teflon-type surfaces. But you don't really need the steel wool for conventional surfaces either. If food sticks, sprinkle a couple of tablespoons of baking soda on the burnt part and add a small amount of hot water. It should be soft enough to clean in a half hour. If a spot is stubborn, let it soak overnight; it'll be mush in the morning.

Hands won't get burned if you buy a long-handled brush. Take care to work out any food lodged in the ridges of pots or lids. Use a fork handle, if necessary, to push food out, and force in a brush or scrubber to wash.

Rinse all soap off with cold water preliminary to warm rinses. A number of such cold washes will remove the bulk of the soap. They'll save hot water and insure that it will do some good. The last step is to immerse utensils in scalding water, or pour it over them. Only that will kill any remaining germs.

When you have to bring water into a rustic campsite and have little to spare for washing, the practice of prewiping and using a number of washes in small amounts is especially important. If you have no water at all to spare, you can wipe off the excess food and pack all your dirty dishes into a plastic bag to be washed later. Often when I stopped at a park or wayside rest stop for lunch, I'd heat water for tea and to wash the previous night's dishes.

Don't bother to wipe after washing. Just leave dishes upside down on the table to air dry. In my experience, the condition of towels on typical trips—molding inside of soiled panniers or damp and sour in plastic—makes air drying considerably more hygienic. If you feel that you absolutely must use a towel, at least strap it outside of your pack during the day and let the sun freshen it.

When in an organized campground, dump your dishwater into the sink or flush toilet, if it can take it or if it's connected to a sewer. Many camps designate an area where dishwater may be dumped. In the woods or open ground, the likelihood of other campers using the same spot are remote. Your biodegradable dishwater and grease, left on the ground and covered with earth, will be a negligible contribution. The ecologically minded may be shocked by this advice. But bird droppings, animal carcasses, and leaves make more rot than your pittance. It all goes back to the earth—is eaten by insects or becomes humus—soon enough. Cart out paper, certainly; drop it and your cans in the nearest roadside barrel or carry them to the next village.

Many campers use plastic or paper plates and utensils to avoid the bother of dishwashing. These aren't very practical if you're traveling lightly. They're not available in small lots, and if you buy a dozen the rest will have to be carried. Besides, it would seem that we'd want to spare both the forest resources and energy required to make these products.

All cans, as well as waxed and plastic milk cartons, may be saved and used for disposal of grease. Never pour grease on the ground in organized camps. It's unsanitary, it attracts varmints, insects, and even worse in bear country. Don't think that your little bit doesn't count. In contrast to the situation in remote woods, a hundred campers concentrated in a small area soon can have it smelling like a cesspool with such accumulated slop, if each dumps just a little. Policing and cleanliness should not be left to camp custodians; in most places they only empty garbage cans.

The basic responsibility for sanitation lies with the individual camper, not with the hired help.

Food can be stored overnight in one of several ways. The simplest is to take it with you into the tent or bivvy sack. Small animals, even coyotes and raccoons, will not bother you. My only mishaps occurred when I was away from the tent or when food was left in panniers on the bike overnight.

When you take food with you into a tent, seal in its aroma by using plastic bags and tying them well. You might need two bags with an odorous food like cheese. At the least, it will save you from being awakened by a stray dog or cat poking around your tent.

In bear country, you'd better not have food, or even a trace of its scent, anywhere near yourself. A common precaution is to hang it in a net bag from a limb or from a rope drawn between two trees. But don't count on food being safe there. I've heard countless stories of clever responses by bears and other animals to this tactic. Bears were reported to gnaw through the rope that held the food, while squirrels and other climbers were known to shimmy down the rope, chew through the bag, and jump to the ground when through eating. I've also been told that bears get enraged when food is just out of their reach, and go on a rampage through the camp as a consequence.

My practice is to stay out of the wild when bears are in the area, and to use either an indoor facility or an organized camp with a formal sanitation program. In this kind of camp cleanliness is a religion. All garbage is kept in plastic bags and disposed of before dark. Garbage cans are stored in an office building after dark. When these precautions are taken, bears stay away. They know from past rummaging experience that there's no food to be had.

In some campgrounds I stayed at, the management provided latched storage boxes. They were convenient and strong enough to keep out any intruders. If the worst you expect during the night would be chipmunks or mice, pile all the food under up-ended pots. To keep animals from moving them, strap the pots down with shock cords. A few of these can be connected and passed under the table or around a seat to make a tight belt.

Don't depend on bottled or waxed containers to stop pilfering.

Bottles can be pushed off tables and broken. One morning I found a milk carton opened at its pour spout and some of the milk gone. The telltale dirt from an animal's muzzle was there at the opening. Only the clever paws of a raccoon could have done that!

When smaller flying creatures—flies, bees, yellow jackets—bother you at the table, give them their own dirty pot to eat from, off to the side. They'll appreciate it and reward you by feasting alone.

Aside from security considerations, you may want to keep certain foods cool overnight: eggs, milk, breakfast meats. In my experience, most nights have been cool enough so that spoilage was not likely. Milk and eggs that were bought cold in the evening were still cool in the morning, unless the night was unusually hot.

If a stream is handy, food can be placed in it, after enclosing it in watertight plastic. The chances of amphibious animals bothering it would be small. The simplest thing to do in hot weather, though, is either to ask the camp director to hold these items for you in his refrigerator or just not buy perishables for use the next morning.

In the morning the urge is strong after the final clean-up, to throw everything into the packs randomly and to get on the road. But you may have a reckoning that evening, if you arrive in the dark or get caught in the rain and have to search frantically for things. Put everything away systematically—always.

# Cooking for One

As any bachelor can tell you, the problem with solo cooking is shopping. It's often simply impossible to buy, for example, just four ounces of meat, a cup of peas and two pieces of pimento. If you need a stalk or two of celery in your recipe, what do you do with the rest of the bunch?

You could find yourself in a situation where you'd be cooking just for yourself, yet traveling with others. Some groups prefer that each member cook on his or her own. Personally, I see little sense in this arrangement. If it is the case, though, at least shopping could be shared to ease the logistics of getting small amounts of ingredients.

But if you're truly alone, your repertoire is severely limited. You need more ingenuity to seek out food sources, to wheedle small amounts from grocers, and to use substitutes and shortcuts.

A butcher shop or delicatessen counter at a supermarket, when they can be found, are good sources of cooked beef, turkey, assorted meats, and cheeses. The counter person will give you the thickness and amount of meat that you need, if you insist. His slicer can adjust to an inch or more; if it doesn't he can always slice a thick piece with a knife.

In most stores we have to select from either mixes or dried, precooked ingredients. This is unfortunate because so many of these contain EDTA, sodium nitrite, and other chemical villains, and because the taste of factory prepared food is never quite as good as fresh.

Traveling alone you'd carry the standbys—rice, pasta, and cheese—and other lightweight items such as dehydrated parsley, celery flakes, minced onion, potato flakes (although whole potatoes are often available loose and a few at a time can be bought), soup mixes, and powdered milk.

There may be no fresh meats at all in the small grocery where you'd stop. You'd have to buy small cans of boned chicken, Vienna sausage, chunk turkey, Spam, or corned beef. Chipped beef is also a good choice. It's light and will keep a long time, even if you have to buy a large jar of it.

Weights of these canned meats range from five to seven ounces, including water or juices. Throw these liquids out: the balance in the can is enough for a single portion. Meat from a larger can may be saved for a sandwich the next day, given a cool night to keep it fresh. Or a neighbor in a Winnebago may keep it for you in his refrigerator overnight.

Keep in mind that you can always use some of what you buy to make the morning's meal. For example, most of a ham slice can be used to make a rice with ham recipe and the rest can be fried with eggs the next morning. Part of a quart of buttermilk can go into Mexican cumin at night and pancakes at breakfast, then be the beverage at lunch.

If you're forced to buy a canned meal—spaghetti, beef stew, hash—stir in a spice before heating to vary the flavor (1/8 t. per can, unless otherwise noted). Good combinations are basil with tomato dishes; chili powder with corn; tarragon with chicken or fish; oregano with meats and tomato; thyme in soups; sage with pork (a dash); chives (1/4 t.) mixed into eggs and soft cheeses; onion flakes with most dishes (1/4 to 1/2 t.), and a pinch of garlic added to almost anything.

Unless you have no other option, buying the small packages of cooked meat makes little economical or nutritional sense. They're packed in preservatives and padded with fillers, and the cost is two or more times that of fresh meat. You're better off to buy the pound of boneless chicken breast rather than pay the same amount for a can of chicken in which the meat itself weighs just four ounces. Cook the whole pound of chicken, have a feast, and give some to the stray dog or cat that always seems to hang around the camp begging. You'd still have the better of the bargain for the relative purity and better taste of the fresh meat.

When crowded into a corner like that, my shopping habit is to choose the more expensive specialties—the oysters, creamed herring, frozen trout, or shrimp—rather than the slightly less expensive but plebeian canned turkey or Spam. I feel that if I'm to pay through the nose anyhow, I may as well enjoy it.

Because you will carry so few pots when alone, your supplies need to be carefully organized. Your pots will have to do for all operations. On a long trip, I bring a three-quart pot and its deep cover. This pot may seem a bit large for one person, but it happens to fit exactly over the rolled tent I carry in back of my bike. A smaller pot would be awkward to pack away inside my panniers.

I make my meal in one of these two vessels, depending on the amount needed. When I use the cover to make the meal, and the recipe calls for a lid, I fit the larger pot over it.

The cooking sequence may go like this. Perhaps I'm making a chili con carne. I put water on immediately for tea. While it's coming to a boil I use my measuring cup—before I get it wet—to set aside one-half cup of rice on a piece of paper. I then make my tea in the same cup.

I've marked my bike's water bottle on the outside by quarter cups and I use it to pour a cup and three-eighths of water into the bigger pot, adding rice, oil, and a pinch of salt. While the rice is steaming, I chop onion and measure out the rest of the ingredients. When cooked, I put the pot of rice, uncovered, into a paper bag and insert it inside my sleeping bag to keep it warm.

I next make my main dish in the cover, starting with browning the meat and onion, and following the recipe. I pour the cooked chili over the rice and immediately rinse the lid with cold water. Next I put more water in the lid and onto the stove to be warmed.

I'm almost finished eating when the water reaches a boil, and I add soap and wash the lid; now I need more water to boil for a second cup of tea, and so on. The key is washing the big pot and utensils and putting things away as I go along. The stove is used continually and the stages of cooking, eating and cleaning are integrated. I'm not stuck for want of a pot or utensil and not left with as big a cleaning job.

Other dishes might require another sequence. At the outset a few minutes should be spent reading the recipe thoroughly and organizing oneself.

Meals for the first day or two of a trip can be precooked at your home. If you concentrate on meats, or the parts of meals that contain little water—meatballs or Italian sausage with thick tomato sauce, for example—the weight penalty will not be too great. Make your rice or pasta later during the trip to complete the meal.

More elaborate preparations are homemade beef jerky or other dried foods. But this gets you into the realm of dehydrated and freeze-dried foods. These would do if nothing else is available and if you can stand the extra cost. I'd reserve that option only for an emergency ration, ordinarily.

Loneliness on a solo trip always seems to be underscored by solitary cooking. It's the time when you'd not only want to share a meal with someone but also the day's events. But there are those sweet interludes, infrequent and therefore treasured all the more, when another lone traveler crosses your path. Everything expands then: use of cooking implements, the scope of recipes, and the good digestion coming from shared company.

# Cheap or High on the Hog?

Bike touring can be cheap or expensive, depending on the kind of trip you're taking and the amount in your pocket. Yours might be a two-week vacation with cooking an incidental concern. You may enjoy eating informally outdoors, and making your own meals may be just plain fun. Or you might like the feeling of self-reliance that comes with cooking for yourself.

To another person with a tight budget, cooking costs may be a critical factor on a long journey. Since he'd be watching his pennies, he would have to watch his nutrition too, making sure not to short-change the needs of his body.

But food need not be expensive to be good for you. As nutritionists point out, the most affluent people can be undernourished. The snacks and rich desserts they can afford are often eaten in place of foods with essential vitamins and minerals. The four-dollar-a-pound steak of the rich man could actually be a poorer source of protein than the cheap organ meat of a slum dweller. You don't have to eat badly when you go cheaply.

Constant snacks of junk food and expensive cuts of meat are major culprits in high food prices. Snacks can be cut out, but most people—those who do little cooking especially—are loath to give up their chops and steaks. I've observed that as such people learn more about cooking they get weaned away from their steaks. Their tastes tend to become more cosmopolitan; they learn to appreciate subtleties and combinations of a variety of foods.

Buying cuts of cheaper meat, taking organ meats, which are less popular and therefore cheaper, using meat substitutes, meat extenders, and even doing without meat at all are ways to lower costs. The amount of protein you normally need can still be satisfied with legumes and milk products. The case for the meatless meal and its nutritional ramifications will be made in a later chapter. For the time being, we'll concentrate on costs only.

Muscled meats—chuck, neck, shoulder, breast, shank, or the cuts from the forequarters of the animal—can be softened by treating them with tenderizers. These break down meat fibers and connective tissues. Many people, myself included, don't care for tenderizing through chemical action, claiming that the taste is corrupted. I don't like the somewhat mushy texture that results. But if the process isn't carried too far—a simple matter of watching the time carefully—and if you don't miss the tactile pleasure of biting with teeth into a textural piece of meat, it may satisfy you. Follow the package directions, but lean toward less time.

A more direct method of tenderizing is literally to pound the meat into submission. Beat it with the head of your eight-inch adjustable wrench, a hand-sized stone, or any heavy object. Set the meat on a solid table, of course, and shield it from dirt with a few layers of paper bag. You needn't pound it into the table; just work it enough to break down the tough connective tissue. A series of fast, shallow cuts on the surface of the meat will also do, but don't get carried away with this either.

A marinade also tenderizes tough meat, but not as quickly and effectively as the chemical enzyme. The marinating process does add taste, which the commercial tenderizer usually doesn't. Marinades contain an acid base, to weaken the muscles and tissues of the meat, as well as oils and condiments of some sort. The acidic vinegar, lemon, sour cream, or wine add taste also. Formulas for marinades are listed under "sauces." A commercial French dressing can be used as a marinade too.

Marinades are especially suited to travelers: meat that is bought an hour or more before arriving at the evening camp can be placed with the marinade in a plastic bag. The normal agitation from the vehicle bouncing over the road helps the breakdown process along. One can combine marination with mechanical tenderizing, or course; pound the meat first and then let it soak.

Tough meats can also be stewed, pot roasted, or braised to soften them. Tasty one-pot meals that include various vegetables can be made with such meats. They do take longer to cook, an hour and a half or more. Unless you have time to kill, you'd better not take this culinary path.

Organ meats, such as heart, liver, or kidney, are usually scorned by the steak-oriented housewife, but they cost less and are a rich source of vitamins and minerals. Their taste has character and is more distinctive than many expensive cuts. This taste takes some getting used to for most Americans. Foreign recipes mask the strong flavors by the addition of complementary ingredients.

A meal containing a small amount of meat may be extended by vegetables or pasta, either on the side or in one-pot meals. Much of the great cooking of the world is based on such extensions: Chinese and other Far East cooking uses rice and stir-fried vegetables. Dumplings, potatoes, and root vegetables make up much of northern European fare. Corn and beans are bountiful staples that stretch meat in Mexican and Central American dishes. Pulpy fruit like bananas and pineapple are used widely by Latin Americans and Pacific people. These carbohydrates and sugars can well serve bikers; not only do they supply calories, but they add solid nutrition.

Check the one-pot dish recipe for those special ingredients— nuts, sour creams, mushrooms, pimento—that can easily make the meal as expensive as if you used a choice cut.

Vegetables and fruit have risen astronomically in cost lately, at least in the United States. Overseas, they're still considerably cheaper than meat. In this country, you'd have to weigh the current price of ground meat versus a vegetable like green pepper or cauliflower. You'd want the vegetable for the sake of your diet, but it may approach the meat in price. In the case of cheese, meat is already cheaper. But rice, pasta, and root vegetables are always a good buy; so is almost all fruit when in season. I've found such fruit to be fresher, more apt to be vine or tree ripened, *and* cheaper at roadside stands.

One late summer day near Cambridge, Maryland, I passed farm after farm at which muskmelon were being picked. In the field where the workers were already finished, hundreds of melons were left behind. I assumed they were rotten. But when I stopped for a break I noticed that many of the melons were whole and not rotten at all. They were simply too ripe to be transported. I ate one and it was truly delicious, nothing like the hard flesh of the typical melon from a supermarket. Imagine! Some of the best produce can't even reach the customer.

But the aftermath of that episode was more bizarre. At a stand at a private home I found some of the same kind of melon. It was being sold cheaply. The next day, at an outdoor market in Dover, the price of the melons rose to nearly double. They were firmer there and the smell wasn't as musky as at the stand. Later, at a supermarket outside the same city, melons had a still higher price.

"How come?" I asked the clerk. "Just across town they're considerably cheaper. And it's grown around here, besides."

"These here are from California," he said. He told me the company buyer had control over where they got their fruit. The experience taught me something about the idiosyncrasies of the distribution system.

Bonnie Wong, the bicycle tourist, beats salad prices by growing her own sprouts in plastic containers. When traveling alone, that would be about the only way to get your greens, short of picking them wild. It's hard to use up a head of lettuce, even by four people.

A meat extender that is both economical and rich in protein is soybean. Toasted soya granules cost from one-half to two-thirds of ground meat per pound, and they don't have any fat content. They don't fry down either, a trait that makes them even more of a value. You can mix a quarter pound of the soy with each pound of ground beef. Soya granules need no refrigeration, unlike wheat germ.

To cut costs, substitute more modest items of the same type for expensive ones. Some tastes may be so ingrained that you can't give them up easily. Witness coffee; the cheaper tea doesn't do for many. Still, you can cut down on coffee somewhat. After the price went up a few years ago, I drank only one cup in the morning in protest, and took tea the rest of the day. I like tea now; tastes do change if you give them a chance. Using margarine instead of butter on your bread, and substituting oil for margarine in frying are other ways to economize.

A pernicious shopping habit is buying lunch meats for sandwiches. These are almost as expensive as steaks in many cases. Their nutritive content is no better, and often inferior, to cheese or peanut butter. Substitute the latter for cut meats.

Pre-cooked foods are obviously more expensive to buy. You do expect the producer to charge for the cooking service. But the price on the package may be even worse than it first appears. When you examine the contents you may find that bread crumbs, flour, water, and other cheap ingredients form a substantial part of the package's weight. The price of the main ingredient may be four times that of the food when fresh. Always calculate the actual cost per pound.

Make your own gravies and sauces. Flour, milk, and pan drippings, their basic ingredients, are cheap and don't contain additives. Don't be tempted by the seemingly low price of twenty-five to thirty-five cents for a store package; you can make them for pennies. Prepare your mustard, too, from powder—just add a little water.

Compare the price of shredded cheese with the hard version. Surprisingly, the shredded is sometimes cheaper by weight. If it isn't, shred it yourself. Don't bother with a grater; you can just shave off pieces with a knife.

The additional cost of fancy packages should be apparent to everyone. Yet people still buy a cardboard container printed with pictures, games, and recipes without comparing its price to the less elegant but identical "soft" package of plastic. Rice is an example. There is absolutely nothing a national company can do to rice to improve its quality. It can only buy it from the farmer and package it, with the ordinary precaution to keep it clean.

What follows from the above is that the large name-brand company charges more for the same product. In effect we subsidize the national advertising campaigns. There are varying taste preferences, to be sure, for products partially or extensively prepared. These often work both ways. I find as many cheaper brands whose taste I prefer to the expensive ones as vice versa. In any case, if your experience shows that taste is not a criterion, buy the off brand. Or buy the generic "no brand" foods that are finding their way to grocery shelves lately.

The popular cold cereals of the two or three large grain companies combine all the negative aspects of food purchasing. These name brands are attractively packaged and made ready-to-eat. They're poor buys, however, very much overpriced. Get the supermarket's own brands of cereals that you cook, such as hot oatmeal and farina.

Watch for supermarket specials, those lead items which are intended to draw customers and have them buy their week's groceries at the store. You'd buy only the sales item, of course, perhaps a few others, and get the price advantage.

Buying in large volume in order to save is not especially practical for bikers. The extra amount would have to be carried, perhaps for days, until consumed. It isn't worth the savings unless the group is large enough so that each person can share the burden. There are times when it can be done, though, when you lay over for a few days somewhere or when you meet and camp with another group. Most of the contents can then be used up before getting back on the road.

Forget about freeze-dried foods completely. Many approach the cost of a meal at a diner and taste worse. A freeze-dried meal of eggs with butter costs $1.75, plus shipping, when you buy it by mail from an equipment supplier. That's more than what it would cost you at a restaurant. An eight ounce tuna salad is $2.50. Who needs it? Maybe backpackers, who are truly in the wilderness, but not anyone riding on the road.

Restaurants and fast food outlets can sometimes help you economize on a trip, as strange as that may sound. Only expensive cuts of meat might be available at the local grocery, for example. Rather than settle for these or eat a complete meal at the restaurant, you can buy just the entree—cooked chicken or fish—from a restaurant or a Kentucky Fried Chicken store and make the rest of the meal yourself.

Sometimes, when alone, you might be faced with an expensive campground or a motel as the only formal accommodation available in a congested or high-priced area. The lateness of the hour and a closed grocery may preclude cooking that evening. There would be no particular advantage to staying at a campground; you'd be paying only for ground space.

But there may be plenty of opportunity to find that ground space at no cost in the woods, on a beach, or in a field a short distance out of town. You can then eat a leisurely meal in a restaurant, most likely for less than the cost of a motel or campground. You can dawdle over a book or write letters over cups of tea until it's bedtime, and then retire for the night to your private site. A shower can always be postponed a day and you can make do with a wash in the restroom.

In contrast, when you're in an area known for its cuisine or a special restaurant, you'll probably want to live it up. By all means! Good food is the cheapest and most pleasant way to raise your morale and make the trip memorable. Unlike an expensive room, you carry a fine meal away with you and make good use of it afterwards.

In foreign countries, with a lower cost of living, eating out can well be the norm, or a frequent occurrence. I spent less than $3 a day for restaurant food in Europe and Asia in 1974 and less than that in Poland during two months in 1972. Even allowing for today's inflation, restaurant eating overseas is a bargain. You'd have to choose the restaurant, of course; look for a family type frequented by the middle class of that country rather than one catering to tourists.

Keeping a record of food costs may not make the trip less expensive, but it's essential when traveling with a group. In spite of all fine intentions and good will at the outset, there comes a time when someone becomes either suspicious or resentful of the money holder and calls for an accounting. Not that anyone would gain a fortune by absconding with the funds. It eases minds, though, to have an open and direct accounting system available rather than to depend on someone's memory. And, incidentally, it helps give the group some idea of their spending progress.

Rather than chip in each time the cook would shop for food and pay for the campsite, we would advance him a certain amount, perhaps ten dollars apiece, against which he would draw. He entered each day's expenses in a small notebook, keeping receipts. When he ran out of money, usually in about three days, we'd advance him another sum. Or he'd float us, and we'd square the account at the end of his regime. Whenever a bicyclist joined or left the group, we'd settle the debts and start from scratch.

At the end of a cook's tour of duty the assistant would inherit the book. This log was always available to anyone who wanted to see it. We left it on the table with the cooking gear each evening, in fact, to spare any possible embarrassment in asking for it. Any criticism of spending habits could be made by anyone, right on the spot. Not that we ever had any—the tacit control and openness was enough to remove that possible source of conflict.

An indication of the economy possible in group travel in the United States is given by what we spent on our Edge trip in 1977-78. It cost us less than $3.50 a day, apiece, for supper, breakfast and lodging. Food itself was $2.50 a day. About the same was spent in 1976 on a Bikecentennial trip I led. That amount doesn't include personal spending for snacks, beer, or lunches. We bought no junk food—candy, soda, munchies—on a group basis. But we didn't skimp on wholesome food; we ate like horses, in fact.

# Natural Foods

## by June Clifton

*Natural foods*, to me, are those foods that have not been altered too much from their natural state. Examples are: fresh organically-grown vegetables and fruits, unrefined flours and grains, cheeses without harmful preservatives and colorings, raw honey, fertilized eggs, herb teas, and just generally avoiding "junk foods" and factory processed products containing potentially harmful additives.

Traveling by bicycle, or any other mode of transportation, I can usually maintain my standards for nutritious eating through careful planning, and by carrying along pre-packed "natural" foods. I rely heavily on foods such as soy grits, brown unrefined rice and other grains, beans, tamari, fresh vegetables, and good cheese, but occasionally compromises must be made. This is especially true if I travel for several days without finding a so-called natural foods store. In buying at a supermarket, read the labels carefully. Frozen foods are sometimes better than canned because they are less likely to contain additives. Try to buy fruits and vegetables in season, preferably from local vegetable stands. They may not be organic, but they'll be fresh. Sometimes eggs may be purchased from a local farmer; look for "eggs for sale" signs. There might possibly be a mill in the area where you're traveling. This would be an interesting stop as well as a good source of flour or cornmeal.

In preparing for your trip, buy foodstuffs that will store easily, are nutritious, and will be useful to you. Some of my choices are: tamari (a soy-based sauce; store in a leak-proof container), or miso (a soy-based paste); vegie-cubes (like bouillon, only all vegetables; great for broth or soup stock); naturally dried fruits (apricots, raisins, etc.); grains and beans that cook quickly (soy grits, short-grained brown or converted rice, bulgur/cracked wheat, buckwheat groats/kasha, oats, lima beans, lentils, mung beans, split peas); alfalfa seeds for sprouting, dried herbs for seasonings and tea; dried fish; oats or granola mixed with non-instant  powdered milk (just add water and dried fruit for breakfast); raw honey; noodles or macaroni. Many of these items are available only in natural food stores. Carry them in air-tight or leak-proof containers.

A *sample pack* might include: a bag of soy grits; a bag of lima beans; a bag of short-grained brown rice; about 20 vegie-cubes; tamari; herbs and spices; honey; a small bag of alfalfa seeds; some dried fruit; safflower oil; and granola mixed with non-instant powdered milk. Non-instant powdered milk is very concentrated thus very nutritious. It doesn't mix well in liquids, so mix it with dry ingredients first. This milk gets lumpy if not stored in an air-tight container. Soy grits or buckwheat groats or bulgur would be a must in my pack. They contain protein, carbohydrates and vitamins, and can be prepared in many ways (see recipes on pg. 137), separately or mixed, and cook in about 15 minutes. Buckwheat groats "stick to your bones." They are also sometimes available in large supermarkets. The granola will keep if all ingredients are well dried (i.e. no fresh, raw nuts). Granola is great for snacks as well as for breakfast.

You might want to package a flour mixture, to be used in preparing pancakes, griddle cakes, creamed soups, creamed vegetables, croquettes, etc. This mixture shouldn't be kept more than a week or two if you are traveling in hot weather; it could lose freshness and possibly become rancid. Possible ingredients are: 3 cups of wholewheat flour; one to two cups of any of the following or a mixture (oats, cornmeal, bran, soy flour, wheat germ); 1/3 cup of brewers yeast; one cup of non-instant powdered milk; and one tablespoon of salt.

I am not a meat eater. Some *meat substitutes* or sources of protein are: legumes, grains, wheat germ, brewers yeast, cheese, eggs, yogurt, fresh or non-instant powdered milk, peanut butter, tofu (a soybean curd, good sauteed with vegetables), nuts and seeds, fish, tamari and miso. Legumes and grains eaten together provide an excellent meat substitute. A favorite dish of mine is cooked rice and cooked beans, sauteed with onion in a large pan, then slices of cheese placed on top to melt. Powdered milk, soy flour or brewers yeast added to soups and other dishes provide more protein. Consult Frances Moore Lappe's *Diet for a Small Planet* for complementary protein combinations.

Obviously products such as cheese, eggs, milk and yogurt must be kept cool, but they'll keep a while if purchased shortly before ending the day's travel. Tofu might be difficult; I've only seen it sold in natural food stores and it should be kept covered with water until used. It's a good protein source, though.

Just remember, try to keep it simple in planning and preparing meals. Any evening meal leftovers (potatoes or other vegetables, rice, soy grits, etc.) can be added to pancake batter or omelets for breakfast. Any eggs, milk or cheese left over from the evening meal should certainly be eaten before beginning the day's journey. Don't peel potatoes or pare carrots. It saves time and the skins have valuable nutrients. Just scrub them with water. Try preparing an evening meal with little or no cooking: uncooked vegetables, fruits, canned tuna, bread, yogurt. Make a quick soup or broth using vegie-cubes or tamari; throw in some buckwheat groats or bulgur.

Proteins are essential to a well-balanced diet. However, long distance bicycling, motorcycling, hiking, cross country skiing, and such activities, call for extra stamina. In order to maintain sufficient fuel for the body in these activities, a diet high in *carbohydrates* is required. Some foods that contain not only protein but a proportionately higher amount of carbohydrates are, in descending order: bulgur, barley, rice, rye, buckwheat, dates, wheat, oats, lima beans, wheat germ, raw soybeans (about equal in protein and carbohydrates), garlic, cashew nuts, sweet potatoes, sweet corn, bananas, sesame seeds, almonds, potatoes, plums, cherries, walnuts, grapes, pears, peas, apples.

*Nuts and seeds*, tasty and high in protein as they are, should be bought often but in small quantities because they can't be stored too long. Due to their high fat content, they could become rancid if the weather is hot and damp. Nuts and seeds are excellent when added to rice and vegetable dishes, used as a garnish with soups, or eaten as a snack as you travel (see recipes on pg. 137).

Try out any *foraging* skills you may have with local wild flowers, plants, nuts, seeds and berries. Depending upon the time of year and location, such plants as wild onion, garlic, leeks, daylilies, nasturtiums, cress, dandelions, lambs quarters, chickweed, purslane, mints and many, many more may be used to supplement meals. I'm no expert by any means, but I have used daylilies, wild onion and garlic, cress and nasturtiums in salads or sauteed vegetable dishes.

*Sprouting* of seeds, beans, or grains tremendously increases their food value. If you carry a small container of seeds to sprout as you travel, once you've developed the habit and established a routine, sprouts could become a relatively inexpensive, tasty and nutritional addition to your diet. I strongly recommend it.

Sprouts can be eaten raw by themselves, in salads, on sandwiches, or as a soup garnish. They can be added to egg omelets, pancakes, steamed or sauteed with vegetables—whatever you might think of.

Buy untreated seeds. Alfalfa seeds, mung beans, lentils, and buckwheat groats are just four of the many possibilities. I prefer alfalfa; a little goes a long way.

Directions for sprouting:
- 2 T. seeds
- water
- qt.-sized jar, preferably with a wide-mouthed opening, and and cover. (You need a lid with small holes punched in it; or a piece of cheese cloth held on either by a rubber band or a metal screw band from a two-piece cap used in canning. Or you might buy a container with lid used specifically for sprouting.)
- After rinsing the seeds and pouring off all the water, lay the jar on its side—at a slight downward angle, if possible.

In the evening put 2 tablespoons of seeds in a jar and cover seeds with water. Allow to stand overnight. In the morning, with lid on the jar, pour off the liquid; put warm water into the jar and slosh around to rinse all the seeds, and then pour off all that water. (You must rinse the seeds at least twice a day; three times a day if the weather is very warm and dry). After pouring off all the water, lay the jar on its side. If possible, lay the jar at a slight angle so any excess water can drain off. Keep the jar in a warm, preferably dark place until sprouts appear. Sprouts can grow in dark or light, but avoid direct sunlight. A good place to keep the jar might be in a handlebar touring bag if you're traveling by bike. Or place it inside your bed roll if not too hot, or strapped on top of your pack with a sandow.

In two to three days alfalfa and buckwheat sprouts will appear; they are ready when about 1" long. Mung beans and lentil sprouts appear in about two days; they are ready when about 1/2" to 1" long. The sprouts should be rinsed and eaten as soon as possible, otherwise they'll lose nutritional value and without refrigeration will spoil.

Making a pot of *soup* can be easy, tasty, and good for you. Using your imagination, soups could be prepared almost every day without becoming boring. If you have some rice or soy grits, for instance, throw either or both into water or stock, cook, then add more liquid and some vegetables and you have a soup. With a soup base (see soup stock below), you can add any grain or vegetable and make a nice soup. Serve bread and salad or carrot sticks with soup and you've got a meal, and only one pot to clean afterwards.

For more protein or just good taste, garnish soups with grated or thinly sliced cheese, sprouts, seeds, nuts, cubed toasted bread, diced hard cooked eggs, herbs, chives, parsley, cress, yogurt, diced green pepper, or whatever you can think of.

Beans and peas will cook faster if they've soaked several hours. If it's possible, after breakfast put beans or peas and water in a leak-proof container and pack it so the beans are always covered with water. Then, use that water as part of the stock since it contains valuable nutrients.

Since it would be almost impossible to have *soup stock* on hand, or to prepare it from scratch while traveling, take a large supply of vegie-cubes, or a container of tamari, or some miso. To make soup stock: to four cups of hot water add one of the following (1/4 cup of tamari; 2 or 3 tablespoons of miso; or two or three vegie-cubes). More may be added to suit your taste.

# PART TWO

# RECIPES

# Meats

All recipes in this book, except those for one-person cooking, are based on four adult diners. Adults will differ in appetite, naturally, and amounts in the ingredients may have to be adjusted accordingly. Recipes with an asterisk are especially suited to use by one person by scaling down the ingredients. Conversely, the ingredients in any one-person recipe can be quadrupled for a group of four.

Some recipes are offered in two or more versions. I've tried to limit that practice to those that differ enough in technique or ingredients to warrant the variation. Where ingredients can be easily interchanged, I list a few short variations with the original recipe, or just leave it up to the cook's imagination to make changes.

A pot is assumed for cooking all dishes unless a skillet is specified. If you have just one container, of course, that will have to do. All cooking is done without a cover unless otherwise specified. You can saute or brown in a pot, or you can use someone's mess kit or fry pan. Nothing in this book is baked, except a few quick breads in a fry pan.

I list oil for frying in almost all cases. Butter and oleomargarine taste better, but oil is easier to carry. If you use a non-stick pan, cut the indicated oil to half or less.

Flour can be of any kind; I use white only, rather than carry others. Cornstarch or arrowroot can substitute for thickening purposes, but flour or bread crumbs are preferred for dredging.

I indicate one teaspoon of salt for the average four-person recipe. Extra salt can always be added during hot weather, high exertion, or to taste. Recipes that contain salty ingredients—soy, chipped beef—could have the salt cut down. Conversely, when ingredients absorb salt readily as do potatoes and other starches, the amount may be increased.

Bring wine vinegar, which can be used in any of these recipes, rather than store an additional kind. When bouillon is called for, dissolve one bouillon cube per cup, or less, of hot water, or buy it in a can if you prefer.

All canned ingredients should be drained of their juices before use, unless otherwise stated. Sizes of cans and packages of frozen vegetables are approximate, since manufacturers' products may vary.

See the appendix for the abbreviations used in the recipes.

Although meats are the richest source of protein in food form, they also have serious shortcomings. They are usually concentrated in saturated fats and filled with chemical additives—those that fatten the animal, that preserve, or that add sales appeal through coloring. None of those do anything for consumers; they bring instead a commercial advantage to the producers. Meats are also the most expensive source of protein and the most wasteful of cereal use.

Yet, even though these facts are accepted, few people raised on meat could come to terms with a completely vegetarian diet as an alternative. They would feel unfulfilled, as if the meal were lacking an essential ingredient. I know the psychological tyranny of that "meat tooth." I have it too.

Still, it's possible to lessen your dependence on meat. You would not harm yourself in any way. Active people, especially, do better with greater proportions of carbohydrates in their meals. And so does your budget, as was pointed out in the chapter on costs.

In this chapter, then, you'll find a goodly representation of the cheaper meats—ground beef, chicken, sausage—and those that lend themselves to extension with vegetables and starches. A brief mention of ways to cook steaks and chops is included also, for those times when you have a surplus in your pocket.

Ground beef may be extended as well, with egg, bread crumbs, ground potato, or soya granules, whether in patty or meatball form. Soya is too dry for direct use. First soak a half cup of it in one cup of water for five minutes before combining with the meat.

Some of the meat dishes take longer to prepare than the average traveler would like to invest. These are the stews, the special involved dishes, or the tougher cuts that take long, low heat to cook, in the vicinity of an hour and a half. I include them for the occasions when you have a short traveling day or when you take a day off. Those meals cost you no extra effort, in most cases, just the extra time to be left on the stove with only a periodic check to see that the flame isn't out.

Tougher meats can be braised. Or they can be marinated, if you have the time and opportunity. (See "marinade" on pg. 161.) To braise, first brown the meat quickly in some of its own melted fat or a bit of oil. Add enough water or beef bouillon to cover the bottom of the pot, about a half to one cup, and simmer until tender. Do not boil. Add more liquid if it steams away. Time depends on the size of the cut and its tenderness, at least an hour for tough beef if not tenderized.

Add vegetables the last thirty to forty minutes. Root types—carrots, onions, potatoes, turnips—go well with braising. Slice them if shorter cooking times are used. Make a gravy of the pan drippings.

For tender meats, you may pan broil. Brown meat in a preheated pan. Lower the heat and cook uncovered until done. Pour off any fat as you go along. If you partially cover the pan, the meat will steam somewhat; that will soften a less than tender cut. Time will be short; perhaps only ten minutes for a beefsteak an inch and a half thick.

Veal and lamb take somewhat less time to cook than beef. Veal is expensive, but lamb can usually be bought at reasonable prices overseas, especially in Moslem lands.

All meat should be tested before declaring it done. Either stick in a fork or cut it close to the bone and examine for color. If it's pink, cook it longer. Complete cooking is critical for pork, less so for other meats. For a tender cut of beef, rare cooking may even be preferred. I've known hardy types who eat raw hamburger.

Recipes with an asterisk (*) are suitable for one-person use, with modification.

# Beef, Veal, and Lamb

### Steak*
3 lbs. tender cut of beefsteak, 1 - 1 1/2" thick

Score fat to prevent curling. Pan broil over medium flame or grill over coals about 8 minutes each side, depending on taste.

### Stir-Fry Beef with Vegetables*

| | |
|---|---|
| 1 lb. beefsteak | 1/2 c. dry wine |
| 3 T oil | 1 beef bouillon cube |
| 2 med. onions, sliced | 1/4 c. hot water |
| 1 clove garlic, minced | 1/4 t. ground ginger |
| 3 med. green peppers | 1 T cornstarch in 1 T water |
| 1 med. zucchini | 1 T soy sauce |
| 1/2 lb. fresh mushrooms | 1 T sugar |
| 2 med. tomatoes | 1 T vinegar |

Slice steak very thinly. Core peppers and slice into thin rings. Slice zucchini and mushrooms, and chop tomatoes coarsely. Preheat oil in pan. Dissolve bouillon in hot water and combine with rest of ingredients in separate container. Stir-fry meat, onion and garlic over medium flame, until the uncooked look of the meat is gone. Add vegetables and continue frying two minutes. Remove steak temporarily. Add sauce to pan and stir well. Simmer covered over low flame until vegetables are just tender but still crisp to the bite—a few minutes. Replace steak and rewarm. Serve over rice. Various other vegetables may be used, either fresh or frozen, adjusting cooking time. With sweet tasting vegetables—carrots, peas—soy may be replaced with 1/2 teaspoon marjoram.

### Spiced Beef with Vegetables

| | |
|---|---|
| 1 1/2 lbs. flank steak, sliced thin | 1/2 c. dry wine |
| | 1/4 c. Worcestershire sauce |

2 t. basil
1 t. garlic powder
2 t. ginger
1 bay leaf
1/4 c. oil

1 lg. onion, sliced
1 pkg. each frozen cut beans,
   broccoli and carrots
2 c. beef bouillon
2 t. cornstarch

Combine liquids, except bouillon and spices, and place in plastic bag, with steak. Marinate 1 hour or more. Cook all vegetables in bouillon, keeping them on the firm side. Stagger starts according to cooking time on packages. When done, set vegetables and liquid aside. Remove and drain steak and discard marinade. Brown steak over medium heat for a few minutes, stirring. Add vegetables and liquid. Stir cornstarch into bouillon and add to meat dish. Cook until sauce is thick. Serve over rice.

**Steak in Pita Bread**

1 lb. thick steak, sliced very
   thin
1/2 wine marinade recipe (add
   1/2 t. oregano)
assortment of chopped vegetables, about 4 c.: greens,

fresh spinach, tomato, celery, onion, cucumber, scallions
4 lg. pita bread sandwiches
4 very thin slices Swiss cheese
1 c. sour cream

Marinate steak slices an hour or more. Drain meat well and discard marinade. Stir-fry over medium flame a few minutes. Divide among sandwiches. Cover with vegetables and finally with cheese and sour cream. Chopped pimento slices may also be added. Serve a rice dish separately if volume is not enough to satisfy appetites.

**Beef Round Steak in Mushroom Sauce**

1 1/2 lbs. beef round 3/4"
   thick
1 lg. onion, sliced thin
1/4 c. flour
1 T oil
1 c. beef bouillon
1 can cream of mushroom
   soup

1 sm. can mushroom pieces,
   drained
1/4 t. tarragon
1 t. salt
1/4 t. pepper

Cut steak into four even pieces. Coat with flour; pound steak into flour. Brown with onion in oil over medium heat a few minutes.

Add bouillon, bring to boil and simmer over low heat, covered, 50 minutes. Stir in the rest and simmer about 10 minutes longer. Serve with rice or potatoes, and vegetables such as cauliflower or spinach.

### Pepper Steak

1 lb. beef chuck or round
   steak
1 clove garlic, minced
1/4 c. oil
1/2 t. salt
1/4 t. pepper
1/4 c. soy sauce
1/2 t. sugar

3/4 c. water
3 stalks celery, chopped
3 green peppers, sliced 1" x 3"
3 tomatoes, cut in 1/8's
4 scallions, chopped
1 T cornstarch in 2 T cold
   water

Slice beef in strips about 1/4" thick. Brown with garlic in oil. Add seasonings, soy, sugar and water and bring to boil. Simmer covered 30 minutes. Add celery and pepper and simmer 10 minutes. Stir in tomato, scallions and cornstarch and simmer 5 minutes. Serve over rice. A cup of bean sprouts may be substituted for celery (add with cornstarch), and onions for scallions.

### Pot Roast with Wine and Vegetables

1 1/2 lbs. chuck steak 1 1/2"
   thick
1 recipe wine marinade, less
   thyme and cloves
1 lg. onion, sliced
1 T oil
1 med. tomato, chopped

1/2 t. marjoram
5 carrots cut in 2" pieces
5 stalks celery, cut 1/2"
5 med. potatoes, quartered
1/2 t. salt
1/4 t. pepper
1 sm. can mushrooms, drained

Marinate meat. Drain and brown with onion. Add marinade, tomato and marjoram and bring liquid to a boil. Cover and simmer over a very low flame for 1 1/2 to 2 hours. At 45 minutes, turn meat over and add vegetables, salt and pepper. Add mushrooms during last 10 minutes. Serve with dumplings or noodles.

### Beef in Beer*

1 1/2 lbs. beef, cubed 3/4"
1/4 c. vinegar

3/4 c. oil
2 med. onions, sliced

1 t. ground mustard
1/2 t. sugar
1/2 t. Worcestershire sauce
1/4 c. water
8 oz. full-bodied beer or malt

1 clove garlic, minced
3 T oil
1 t. salt
1/4 t. pepper
2 T flour

Marinate beef in vinegar and oil on way to campground. Drain meat well and brown with onions and garlic. Add salt and pepper. Stir, in turn, flour, mustard, sugar and Worcestershire sauce into water. Add this mixture to the pan's contents slowly, stirring. Then stir in beer slowly. Bring to boil and simmer about an hour. Top with more beer to cover beef, if necessary. Serve with rice or whole potatoes, and vegetables.

**Beef Stew I**

1 1/2 lbs. stew beef, cubed
    1 1/2"
1 recipe wine marinade
1/4 c. flour
3 T oil
1 lg. onion, sliced
3/4 c. beef bouillon

2 potatoes, sliced 1/4"
1 sm. turnip, diced 3/4"
4-5 carrots, sliced 1/2"
3 potatoes, cubed 1 1/2"
2 t. salt
3/4 lb. fresh or frozen peas

Marinate beef 1 hour or longer. Drain and coat with flour. Brown with onions over medium flame, lightly. Replace marinade and bring to boil for a few minutes. Add bouillon and sliced potatoes and top with water, if necessary, to cover beef. Bring back to boil and simmer covered 1 1/2 hours or longer. Stir occasionally. Add turnip, carrots, cubed potatoes and salt during last 30 minutes. Add peas last 10 minutes, or long enough to cook.

**Beef Stew II**

2 c. cooked rice (cook 10
    mins. only)
1 lb. stew beef, cubed 1"
1 1/2 c. vinegar marinade
    (without bay leaf and
    cloves)
3 T oil
1/8 t. nutmeg

1/8 t. cinnamon
few drops Tabasco
1/4 lb. chipped beef
1 med. onion, chopped
1 lb. can tomatoes
3 pkg. frozen vegetables:
    among kale, okra, corn ker-
    nels, turnips, lima beans

Marinate beef 1 hour or longer. Simmer rice while preparing ingredients for rest of meal. Drain water and set aside for rice. Drain stew beef and discard marinade. Brown beef quickly over medium high heat. Wash chipped beef and cut in 1" pieces. Add chipped beef and onion to pan and saute a few minutes. Add spices and tomato. Top with water if necessary to cover meat. Bring to boil and simmer covered 1 1/2 hours or longer. Add vegetables at intervals before end of cooking, according to package directions and whether fresh or canned. Add half-cooked rice last 15 minutes and stir in well. Salt will probably not be needed if the chipped beef is salty, otherwise salt to taste.

### Irish Stew (from Dennis Devlin)

| | |
|---|---|
| 1 1/2 lbs. stew beef, cubed | 1 bunch carrots |
| 1 1/2" | a few sweet potatoes, if avail- |
| 2 onions, chopped | able |
| 1 clove garlic, minced | a few parsnips |
| 1 bay leaf | 2 qts. water |
| 8 potatoes | |

Combine beef, onions, garlic and bay leaf in water. Bring to boil, reduce to low boil for 30-40 minutes. Add vegetables and cook 30-40 minutes longer. Stir occasionally. If parsnips are used, add last 10-15 minutes. Top with water to just cover, if necessary.

### Beef Stroganoff I

| | |
|---|---|
| 1 1/2 lbs. round steak, cubed | 1/2 t. marjoram |
| 1/2" | 1 c. beef bouillon |
| 1/4 c. flour | 1 lb. fresh peas, or 2 pkg. |
| 1 med. onion, chopped | frozen |
| 3 T oil | 1/2 lb. can mushrooms, |
| 1 t. salt | drained |
| 1/2 t. paprika | 1 c. sour cream |

Dredge meat in flour. Sear meat and onions. Stir in condiments, bouillon, and peas. Simmer 25 minutes, or until meat is done. Add sour cream and mushrooms and heat well without coming to a boil. Serve over noodles and with salad.

## Beef Stroganoff II, Quick

1 1/2 lbs. round steak, sliced
   very thin, in strips 3/4" x 2"
1 med. onion, chopped
3 T oil
1/2 t. Worcestershire sauce

1 can mushrooms, drained
1 lb. can mixed vegetables,
   drained
1 c. sour cream

Pound steak strips to tenderize. Saute over medium flame with onions for 5 minutes. Stir in rest of ingredients except sour cream. Bring to boil, then simmer about 10 minutes. Add cream; heat well. Serve over noodles.

## Corned Beef and Onions (from Ray Ching, Tinton Falls, N.J.)

4-6 onions, sliced
12 oz. can corned beef
1/4 t. pepper

2 T oil
1-2 T soy sauce

Fry onions 2-3 minutes. While still crisp, add broken up chunks of beef. Heat until hot. Add soy and pepper. Serve over rice or eggs, or oriental type noodles. For added flavor and calories, poach eggs on top of beef mix, with the pot covered, a few minutes until firm.

## Corned Beef, Cabbage, and Vegetables

1 head cabbage, shredded
   roughly
water in pan, about 3/4"
a few carrots, diced 1"
1/2 lb. turnips, diced 1/2"
4 onions, quartered lengthwise
3/4 lb. potatoes, cubed 1"

1 T parsley flakes
1/8 t. nutmeg
1/2 t. ground mustard
1 t. salt
1/4 t. pepper
12 oz. can corned beef

Place cabbage in water, then layer rest of vegetables in order. Sprinkle condiments on top, cover well and bring to boil. Simmer 20-25 minutes or until vegetables tender. Add broken up chunks of corned beef, mix contents of pan a bit, and simmer another 5 minutes.

**Corned Beef Hash***

| | |
|---|---|
| 4 lg. potatoes, diced 3/8" | 1 t. Worcestershire sauce |
| 2 onions, chopped | 1 t. salt |
| 12 oz. can corned beef | 1/2 t. pepper |
| 2 T oil | 1/2 t. ground mustard |
| 1/2 c. beef bouillon | 1/2 t. sage |
| 1 can cream mushroom or | |
|   celery soup | |

Cook potatoes until tender but still quite firm, about 15 minutes. Drain. Saute onion and meat a few minutes. Add potatoes and brown a few minutes over medium flame. Dissolve condiments in bouillon and stir into pan contents. Stir in soup, press mixture down gently and heat 10 minutes uncovered. Turn over, stir up and saute another 10 minutes. Four eggs can be slipped onto mixture and poached, covered, the last 10 minutes. To make a single portion, substitute some white sauce for the soup and skip the bouillon. Also, used cooked ham or roast beef slice, diced, instead of corned beef.


**Lo Mein** (from Ray Ching)

| | |
|---|---|
| 1 or more packages of "Oriental Noodle" soup, which have separate flavor packets | 2 or more vegetables: carrots, broccoli, onion, cabbage, sprouts, sauerkraut, or leafy tender types |
| 12-16 oz. canned meat: corned beef, Spam, ham, shrimp, chicken | |

If using raw meat or sea food, saute first in a little oil and then add vegetables (add sprouts, chives or scallion later). Cook meat-vegetable mixture 3 minutes. Note package directions for noodles. Use only half of water called for and add only half of the flavor packet (save rest of it for 1/2 cup broth or to flavor another meal). Add all the noodles, breaking the cluster into quarters. Stir so noodles absorb liquid and get cooked through. Stir occasionally. Cook 5 minutes or until liquid is almost all absorbed. At this point, sprouts, scallions, or chives can be added. Stir and serve. You may find Lo Mein tasty as described, but Chinese like to add hot mustard, vinegar, and soy to taste when devouring this delectable dish. Be sure to mix the hot mustard throughout before eating. To boost volume, make an omelet, cook it somewhat and cut into slivers. Add just before serving.

### Chipped Beef with Cheese and Egg*

| | |
|---|---|
| 6-8 oz. chipped beef | 1 T Worcestershire sauce |
| 2 T oil | 1/2 t. ground mustard |
| 1 qt. can tomatoes | 12-16 oz. American cheese, or |
| 1 t. chili powder | grated sharp cheese |
| 5 drops Tabasco | 4 eggs, well beaten |

Wash beef well. Cover with boiling water, stir a minute and drain. Lightly saute beef in oil a few minutes. Add tomato and condiments. Cover and simmer about 25 minutes, stirring occasionally. Uncover and stir in the cheese, torn in strips. When cheese melts, add a few tablespoons of the tomato mixture to the container of eggs, one at a time, stirring well. Add the eggs slowly to the pot. Continue stirring until mixture thickens. Take care not to boil, removing pot from flame for short intervals if necessary. May be made with hard boiled eggs, chopped, instead of raw eggs. Serve over croutons, crackers, toast, bread, or rice. Without the chipped beef, this makes a rarebit. For one person, use an 8 ounce can tomato sauce instead of tomatoes.

### Cream Chipped Beef for Pasta*

| | |
|---|---|
| 6-8 oz. chipped beef | 1 c. heavy cream |
| 2 T oil | a few slices pimento, diced |
| 1 lb. can tiny peas, or equivalent in frozen | 1/4 t. pepper |
| | 1/2 c. grated cheese |

Wash beef well. Cover with boiling water a minute and drain. Lightly saute in oil. Add peas, stir and add cream, pimento, and pepper. Heat over medium flame until sauce thickens a bit. Serve over pasta, preferably small macaroni such as shells or chariot wheels. Sprinkle with grated cheese. For one person, make a little white sauce instead of cream and skip pimento.

## Liver and Onions*

| | |
|---|---|
| 2 lg. onions, sliced thin | 1/4 c. flour |
| 2 T oil | 1 t. salt |
| 1 lb. beef liver, thin slices | 1/4 t. pepper |

Preheat pan over medium flame. Saute onion until just tender. Reduce heat to medium low, and move onions to edge of pan. Coat liver in flour. It may be first sprinkled with lemon juice, if desired. Fry liver 2 minutes on each side. Add salt and pepper over all, mix quickly, and serve over rice and vegetables.

## Veal Stew

| | |
|---|---|
| 1-1 1/2 lbs. veal for stew, cubed 1" | 1 chicken bouillon cube |
| 1 1/2 c. wine marinade | 4 carrots, sliced 1/2" |
| 1/4 c. flour | 4 potatoes, quartered |
| 2 T oil | 1 turnip, diced 3/4" |
| med. onion, sliced thin | 1 pkg. frozen peas |
| | 1 can mushrooms, drained |

Marinate veal an hour or longer. Drain and coat with flour. Brown with onion until onion is limp. Add marinade and bouillon. Bring to boil for a few minutes. Cover and simmer 1/2 hour. Add carrots, potato and turnip and simmer 1/2 hour longer. Add peas, bring back to boil, and stir in mushrooms and leftover flour, mixed in 2 T water. You may add dumplings on top of bubbling stew at this time. Cover and simmer 10 minutes. Top stew with water if necessary during stewing.

## Veal Marengo

| | |
|---|---|
| 1-1 1/2 lbs. veal for stew, cubed 1" | 1/4 t. pepper |
| 4 sm. onions, quartered lengthwise | 1 clove garlic, minced |
| | 3 T. oil |
| 4 oz. mushroom pieces | 1 T parsley flakes |
| 1/4 c. flour | 1 T celery flakes |
| 1 1/2 c. med. dry sherry | 1 bay leaf |
| 1 t. salt | 1/4 t. thyme |
| | 1/2 sm. can tomato paste |

Saute veal and vegetables lightly. Set aside. Add flour slowly to the oil in the pan. Blend in well, then slowly add wine to make a sauce. Replace meat and vegetables, bring to boil and simmer covered 1 hour or until meat is tender. Serve with noodles and vegetable dishes. Meat may be marinated in the wine, oil, and condiments if not tender.

### Kidneys

Use veal or lamb kidneys, preferably. To prepare, skin outer membrane, cut in two, and remove the white tissue and all fat. Slice crosswise, or in quarters. Kidneys may be parboiled a few minutes to reduce their strong flavor before cooking.

*Sauteed:*

| | |
|---|---|
| 3 ribs celery, chopped | 1 c. chicken bouillon |
| 2 onions, chopped | 1 T cornstarch |
| 2 T soy bacon bits | 4 oz. mushrooms |
| 3 T oil | 1/2 t. Worcestershire sauce |
| 1 lb. kidneys | 1/2 t. salt |

Saute celery and onions until onions just tender. Prepare and quarter kidneys. Saute covered 5 minutes. Add rest of ingredients, mix and simmer 5 minutes longer. Serve over rice.

*Stew:* Follow veal stew recipe on p. 88 (marinade may be skipped) or substitute 1/2 lb. kidney for same amount of veal.

*Kabob:* Alternate sliced bits of kidney, veal meat, small tomatoes, whole mushrooms, and pieces of bacon on skewers. Baste with French dressing as you broil. When bacon is fried crisp, kidneys are also done. May be seasoned with lemon juice and mustard.

### Lamb Curry

| | |
|---|---|
| 1 1/2–2 lbs. lamb, cubed 1" | 1 lg. yam, cubed 3/4" |
| 1 T oil | 1 lb. potatoes, quartered |
| 2 lg. onions, sliced | 2 pkgs. frozen peas and carrots |
| 2 t. salt | handful of raisins |
| 1/2 t. pepper | 2 apples, cut in chunks |
| 1 T curry powder | 1 T cornstarch |
| 1/4 t. ground ginger | 1 c. plain yogurt |
| 1 1/2 c. beef bouillon | |

Brown meat and onions. Stir in condiments, bouillon, yam and potatoes. Top with water if liquid doesn't almost cover solids. Simmer covered 30 minutes. Stir occasionally. Add vegetables, thawed or frozen, bring to boil, and cook according to package directions. Add raisins and apples and simmer 5 minutes longer. Mix cornstarch in 1 tablespoon cold water and add to stew, along with yogurt. Heat well until thickened, without bringing to a boil.

## Lamb-Soy Meatballs

1 c. soy granules
1 lb. ground lamb
1 egg, beaten
1 t. onion powder
1/8 t. garlic powder
1/4 t. coriander
1 t. salt
1/4 t. pepper
1 T oil

1 can onion soup
1/4 t. each, marjoram, rosemary
1/2 t. salt
2 pkgs. any frozen vegetables
4 potatoes, diced 1/2"
1 T parsley
1 c. plain yogurt

Soak soy 5 minutes in 2 cups water. Combine first 8 ingredients and form into 1" meatballs. Brown well on all sides. Add rest, except vegetables and yogurt, and simmer over very low heat 30 to 40 minutes, covered. Add vegetables and bring to boil. Reduce to low simmer and cook according to longest time on package directions. Stir in yogurt and heat well. Serve over rice.

## Meat Curry (from Rosemary Smith, Sydney, Australia)

1 lb. meat, diced
1 T butter or oil
1 onion, chopped
4 cloves garlic, minced
1 t. fresh or root ginger
1 T fresh parsley, or other
  herbs

1 t. turmeric
1 t. garam-masala (see below)
1/2 t. chili powder (more for
  a hotter curry)
1 t. salt
3 tomatoes, sliced
up to 1 c. water

Remove excess fat from meat. Fry onion, garlic, ginger, and herbs in butter. Add garam-masala, turmeric, chili, and salt and let it sizzle for a few minutes. Add meat and stir a little longer. Add tomatoes and cook over low heat. Water may be added if the mixture becomes dry or a thinner sauce is required. Cook 30-60 minutes, depending on the size and tenderness of the meat. Serve over rice.

*To make garam-masala:*

2 oz. black peppercorns
2 oz. coriander seeds
1 1/2 oz. caraway seeds
(preferably black)

1/2 oz. cloves
20 or more large cardamoms
1/2 oz. cinnamon, ground

Remove skins from cardamoms. Mix with peppercorns, coriander, caraway, and cloves. Grind fairly fine but not powdery. Use a coffee grinder if possible. Mix in cinnamon. Keep in an airtight jar.

**Curry variations**

*Vegetables:* Add at the same time as the tomatoes: mushrooms, peas, potatoes, carrots, etc.

*Fish:* Cod or other fleshy types. Use 1 lb. filleted, well-washed fish cut into pieces, keeping the skin on. Cook herbs and spices as for the meat, but with only 2 cloves garlic and no ginger. Add tomatoes and 2 tablespoons milk-curd (or yogurt) and cook 4-5 minutes. Gently mix in the fish and cover with the sauce. Simmer for 7-10 minutes.

*Eggs:* Boil 8 eggs for 10 minutes, shell, and cut lengthways. Cook herbs and spices as for meat, leaving out the garlic and ginger. Add 1 teaspoon desiccated coconut with the garam-masala and 2 tablespoons milk curd with the tomatoes. Place eggs carefully into the gravy and let it simmer for 10 minutes.

*Cold meat:* Chop 1 lb. meat, removing excess fat. Use any kind, including cold chicken. Cook as for the egg curry.

# Ground Beef

**Hamburgers**

about 1 1/2 lbs. ground beef
1 onion, chopped
1 egg, beaten

1/2 c. bread crumbs, or 1 sm.
grated potato, uncooked
3 T yogurt or milk

1 t. salt                              1/4 t. of thyme, basil, oregano
1/4 t. pepper                          or nutmeg, if desired

Mix all ingredients. Soy granules may be substituted for bread crumbs (soak 5 minutes in 1 cup water first). Extenders and yogurt may be omitted. Form into patties the size of hamburger buns and about 3/4" thick. Oil is generally not needed, but if meat is very lean, you might sprinkle a few drops on the pan. Sear the patties quickly on both sides over moderately high flame to lock in juices, then turn heat down very low. Simmer covered from a few minutes to 10, depending on amount of doneness desired. Serve with buns, cover with various ingredients and serve side dishes.

## Hamburger Variations

*Garlic:* After searing the patties, remove them from the pan and drain excess fat. Saute 3 garlic cloves, minced. Replace patties and continue cooking. Serve over Italian or French bread.

*Cheese Sauce:* To a white sauce recipe, add 1 cup shredded Swiss or a sharp cheese, 1/2 teaspoon dry mustard and 3 tablespoons dry wine. Stir until all is blended and cheese melted. Pour over hamburgers in bun.

*Cheese and Green Pepper:* Saute chopped green pepper in 1 tablespoon oil until just tender. Add to basic recipe, along with 1/4 cup shredded cheese, and shape into patties. Top with a slice of American cheese on each patty in last few minutes of frying, if desired.

*Bacon Bits:* Add 2 tablespoons bacon-flavored soy bits to each pound of meat in basic recipe.

## Chili Con Carne

1 lb. ground beef                      2 cans tomato soup
1 lg. green pepper, chopped            2-3 t. chili powder
1 clove garlic, minced                 1/4 t. cumin
1 lg. onion, chopped                   1/4 t. thyme
1 1/2-2 lbs. canned kidney             1 t. salt
   or pinto beans, drained             1 t. sugar

Brown beef, pepper, and garlic. Drain fat. Stir in the rest. Simmer 30 to 40 minutes, stirring occasionally.

## Ground Beef, Beans and Cheese

1 lb. ground beef
1 onion, chopped
1 can tomato soup
1 t. salt
1/4 t. basil
1/4 c. water
1 pkg. frozen cut beans,
    thawed

4 c. cooked noodles (cook 3
    minutes less than called for)
dash ground cloves
4 slices American cheese, or
    Swiss, torn into strips

Brown beef and onions. Break up clumps. Drain. Add rest, except cheese strips, and stir well. Bring to near boil. Lay cheese strips on top. Cover and simmer on low heat about 25 minutes, or until beans are tender.

## Mexican Ground Beef

1/2 lb. bacon
3/4 lb. ground beef
1 onion, chopped
1 green pepper, chopped
1 pt. tomato juice
1/4 c. corn meal
1 pkg. frozen corn, thawed
1 t. salt
1/4 t. pepper

1/2 t. ground mustard
1 t. chili powder
1/4 t. cumin
1/2 t. oregano
2 eggs, beaten
1/2 t. Worcestershire sauce
1/2 lb. grated sharp cheese
6 green olives, diced

Fry bacon crisp. Set aside and drain pan. Saute beef, onion and pepper a few minutes. Drain. Add rest of ingredients except last four. Mix well, bring to boil, and simmer covered 30 minutes. Mix last ingredients separately in bowl. Add bacon, broken into bits, and pour over the pot contents without stirring. Simmer uncovered until cheese melts and eggs are set. Imitation soy bacon may be used. Serve over rice if you need more volume.

## Sloppy Joe*

1 lb. ground beef
1 lg. onion, chopped
2 green peppers, chopped
1 can tomato soup

1 T ground mustard
1 t. salt
1/4 t. pepper
6 drops Tabasco

Brown beef and vegetables over medium flame. Drain well. Add rest, stir, and bring to boil. Simmer covered until sauce thickened, about 30-45 minutes. Serve over hamburger buns and with big salad. For single person substitute 8 oz. can tomato sauce in place of soup.

## Ground Beef and Celery*

1 lb. ground beef
3 ribs celery, chopped
1 med. onion, sliced thin
1 c. beef bouillon
1/4 c. ketchup

1/2 t. salt
1/4 t. pepper
2 t. Worcestershire sauce
1/2 t. ground mustard

Brown meat slightly. Drain. Add celery and onion and saute until celery almost tender. Drain fat. Add rest and mix well. Serve over noodles or rice.

## Ground Beef and Vegetables

1 lb. ground beef
1 c. beef bouillon
2 pkgs. frozen mixed vege-
    tables
4 potatoes, diced 1/2"

2 t. salt
1 onion, chopped
1/4 t. pepper
2 t. chili powder
1/2 t. oregano

Brown beef and onion and drain. Add bouillon and vegetables, bring to boil. Add rest of ingredients and simmer covered 15 minutes or until potatoes are done. Substitute 8 oz. can tomato sauce and skip vegetables if cooking for one.

## Ground Beef, Macaroni and Cheese*

1 lb. ground beef
3 ribs celery, cut diagonally
1 onion, chopped
1 pt. spaghetti sauce
3 c. water

12 oz. macaroni
2 t. salt
1/4 t. pepper
few drops Tabasco
8 slices American cheese

Brown beef, celery and onion. Drain. Add rest of ingredients except cheese. Bring to a low boil. Cook according to macaroni package directions, stirring frequently. Add water if sauce starts getting too thick. When macaroni is nearly tender add cheese. Cook until it melts into mixture.

## Spiced Ground Meat

1 1/2 lbs. ground beef
6 oz. orange juice
1 t. hot pepper seeds
3/4 t. oregano
3/4 t. tarragon
1/4 t. grated orange peel

2 t. salt
1/2 t. pepper
3 onions, chopped
3/4 c. ketchup or chili sauce
3/4 c. raisins

Brown ground meat and drain. Add orange juice, pepper, and condiments. Stir and bring to boil. Simmer covered 5 minutes. Add orange peel, onions, and ketchup. Simmer 15 minutes, stirring occasionally. Add raisins and simmer 5 minutes. Serve over plain rice. Precooked ground pork may be substituted.

## Ground Beef and Noodle Mix

1 lb. ground beef
1 lg. onion, chopped
1 qt. tomato juice
1 c. water
1 T Worcestershire sauce
1 t. salt
1/4 t. pepper

1/4 t. oregano
1/8 t. thyme
1/8 t. garlic powder
12 oz. noodles, or wide macaroni
1 c. plain yogurt, or sour cream

Brown meat and onion and drain. Add rest except noodles and yogurt. Stir, bring to rapid boil and add noodles. Lower heat to fast simmer, cover and cook 30 minutes or until pasta is done. Stir fairly often to keep pasta from clumping. Take off stove, and stir in yogurt well.

## Ground Beef Stroganoff*

1 lb. ground beef
1 med. onion, chopped
1 clove garlic, minced
1 can mushrooms, drained
1 t. salt
1/4 t. pepper

1 T parsley flakes
1 can mushroom soup
1 t. Worcestershire sauce
1 T flour, dissolved in 1 T cold water
1 c. sour cream

Brown beef lightly over medium heat. Drain. Add onion, garlic and mushrooms and saute 5 minutes. Add rest except cream. Bring to near boil and simmer about 8 minutes. Add sour cream and heat well without boiling. Serve over noodles. Use a little white sauce, instead of soup and cream, and skip the flour for solo cooking.


## Ground Beef with Fruit*

1 lb. ground beef
2-3 lg. onions, sliced
1 c. beef bouillon
2 potatoes, sliced
1 1/2 t. salt
1/4 t. pepper

1/2 t. cinnamon
2 ripe peaches, sliced
2-3 lg. purple plums, or 4-5
    small plums, sliced
2 pears, sliced
1/2 c. raisins

Brown beef lightly. Drain fat. Saute onions with meat. Add bouillon, potato, and condiments. Mix, cover and bring to boil. Cook at fast simmer 20 minutes, or until potatoes almost done. Add rest, except raisins. Fruit should be quite ripe. Slice fruit directly into pot, starting with firmest fruit and adding softest last. Cook until fruit starts becoming soft. Add raisins and mix in well. Serve over plain rice.


## Ground Beef Chop Suey

1 lb. ground beef
1 lg. onion, chopped
3 ribs celery, cut diagonally
    3/8"
1 sm. green pepper, chopped
3/4 c. beef bouillon
1 sm. can water chestnuts,
    drained and sliced
1 pkg. frozen pea pods, or
    green beans, thawed

1 can bean sprouts, drained
1 can mushrooms, drained
2 t. sugar
1/4 c. soy sauce
1/2 t. ground ginger
1/4 t. pepper
2 T cornstarch
2 T cold water

Saute beef lightly. Drain well. Add onion, celery and pepper. Saute until celery near tender. Drain. Add rest, except cornstarch. Bring to near boil, then simmer covered 10 minutes. Dissolve cornstarch in water and stir in. Serve over rice.

## Meatballs and Eggplant

1/2 c. soy granules
1 c. hot water
1 onion, chopped fine
1 16 oz. can tomatoes
1 eggplant, peeled and cubed
   3/4"
3 stalks celery, chopped
1 t. salt

1/4 t. pepper
1 lb. ground beef, lean
1 egg, beaten
1 clove garlic, minced
1 t. oregano
1/2 t. basil
1/4 t. thyme
1/4 c. shredded sharp cheese

Soak soy in water 5 minutes. Combine with beef, egg, and onion and form into meatballs 1 1/2" diameter. Brown over medium flame and drain. Add rest of ingredients, except cheese. Bring to boil and simmer covered 20 minutes. Sprinkle cheese over mixture and heat uncovered until cheese melts. Serve over rice.

## Swedish Meatballs

1 lb. ground beef
1 onion, minced
1/2 c. bread crumbs, or 1
   grated potato, raw
1 egg, beaten
1 t. salt

1/2 t. paprika
1/4 t. nutmeg
1 can cream of mushroom or
   celery soup
1/4 c. dry wine

Combine all ingredients except soup and wine. Make into balls 1" diameter. Brown on all sides and drain. Add soup and wine, bring to near boil and simmer covered 15 minutes. Serve over mashed potatoes or plain rice.

## Chinese Meatballs*

1 lb. ground beef
2 onions, chopped fine
1/4 c. bread crumbs
1 egg, beaten
2 T parsley flakes
4 oz. can mushroom pieces,
   drained
1 t. salt
1/4 t. pepper

1 T cornstarch
1/4 c. water
3 ribs celery, sliced diagonally
1/4 c. sugar
15 oz. can crushed or chunk
   pineapple, unsweetened
1/4 c. vinegar
1/4 t. ground ginger
2 T soy sauce

4 scallions (use whole), sliced
    1/4"
1 green pepper, cut 1/2"
    square

1 T butter
lg. tomato, cut in chunks
2 oz. toasted almonds

Mix first 8 ingredients and make into meatballs 1 1/2" diameter. Brown on all sides and drain fat. Mix cornstarch in water and add to pot. Add celery, pineapple juice, sugar (skip if juice is sweetened), vinegar, ginger, and soy. Bring to boil and simmer covered 15 minutes. Add pepper and simmer covered 10 minutes or until near tender but crisp. Stir in butter, pineapple solids, and tomato, and simmer 5 more minutes. Serve over plain rice and sprinkle with almonds. For single person, use 8 oz. can pineapple, a few fresh mushrooms, and celery flakes, and skip egg.

**Meat Balls for Spaghetti**

3/4 lb. ground beef
1 sm. onion, chopped fine
1/2 c. bread crumbs
1 egg, beaten
1 t. salt

1/2 lb. ground pork
1/4 t. pepper
1/4 t. basil
pinch ground garlic powder
1 pt. spaghetti sauce

Mix all ingredients except sauce and form into 1 1/2" balls. Brown over medium flame on all sides. Drain fat and simmer in spaghetti sauce, covered, 20-30 minutes.

**Meat Sauce for Spaghetti**

3/4 lb. ground beef
1/2 lb. ground pork
1 med. onion, chopped

1 clove garlic, minced
1 pt. spaghetti sauce
1/4 t. oregano

Brown meats, onion and garlic. Drain well. Add sauce and oregano and bring to boil. Simmer 20-30 minutes, covered.

**Golabki (stuffed cabbage)**

2-3 lb. head of cabbage
1 lb. ground beef
1 onion, chopped
1 1/2 c. cooked rice

2 eggs, beaten
1 t. salt
1/2 t. pepper

1 t. poultry seasoning, or Worcestershire sauce
2 c. tomato soup

6 oz. can tomato puree
1 T sugar
1 T vinegar

Place cabbage in large pot of boiling water and let boil about 3 minutes. Drain and let cool until you can separate leaves. Brown meat and onions lightly and drain fat. Mix meat well with rice, eggs, and seasonings. Wrap about 1" balls of meat into the leaves. Roll and fold ends under to hold together and place in pot in layers. Cover with tomato, sugar and vinegar mixture. Bring to boil and simmer covered 1 hour. Baste with sauce occasionally.

# Frankfurters

### Franks and Beans I*

1 lb. frankfurters, cut 3/4"
2 lbs. canned Boston baked
beans
1 lg. onion, sliced thin
1 T Worcestershire sauce

2 T ground mustard
1/4 c. water
4 slices American cheese, torn
into strips

Mix all ingredients except cheese; mix mustard in water first. Cover and simmer 10 or more minutes. Lay cheese on top until melted. Spoon over buttered bread or New England brown bread.

### Franks and Beans II

1 lb. frankfurters, cut 3/4"
2 lbs. canned pork and beans,
chick peas or lentils
2 T oil
1/2 lb. pepperoni, Polish
sausage or other sausage,
sliced thin

1/4 c. ketchup or chili sauce
1 T ground mustard, dissolved
in 2 T water
6 drops Tabasco
1/2 t. salt

Brown franks in oil over medium flame. Add rest of ingredients, stir, and heat well. Use cooked sausage, otherwise precook.

### Franks and Beans III

| | |
|---|---|
| 1 lg. onion, chopped | 1 lb. frankfurters, cut 3/4" |
| 1 med. green pepper, cut in 1/2" strips | 1 1/2 lbs. canned kidney or pinto beans, drained |
| 1 T oil | 1 can tomato sauce |
| 6 oz. can tomato paste | 1/2 c. sharp cheese, shredded |
| 2 t. chili powder | |

Saute vegetables in oil until somewhat tender. Add rest of ingredients except cheese. Heat well and simmer about 10 minutes. Stir in cheese. Serve when melted.

### Franks and Cabbage

| | |
|---|---|
| 1 head of cabbage, cut crosswise to shred roughly | 1 lb. potatoes, cubed 1" |
| water 3/4" deep in pan | 3-4 carrots, sliced 1" |
| pinch ground cumin | 1 t. salt |
| 1 lg. onion, sliced | 2 T oil |
| | 1 lb. frankfurters, cut 1" |

Place cabbage in water. Sprinkle cumin on top. Add vegetables and salt, and sprinkle with oil. Cover, bring to boil and simmer 15 minutes. Stir in franks. Simmer another 10 minutes, or until carrots done.

### Franks and Sauerkraut in Beer (from Ray Ching)

| | |
|---|---|
| 1 lb. frankfurters, cut 1" | 12 oz. beer |
| 1 med. onion, sliced | 2 T ketchup |
| 1 T oil | dash or two Tabasco |
| 1-2 lbs. sauerkraut, drained | 1 t. ground mustard |

Saute franks with onion until light brown. Add rest, mix, and let cook until liquid is almost gone and thickened. Use medium flame. Serve with crusty bread, potato pancakes, and apple sauce.

### Frankfurter Spaghetti

| | |
|---|---|
| 1 lb. frankfurters, sliced 1/2" | 8 oz. can tomato sauce |
| 1 onion, chopped | 1/2 t. salt |
| 1 T oil | 1/2 t. oregano |
| 1 can tomato soup | 1/4 t. thyme |

Brown onions and franks. Add rest of ingredients and bring to boil. Simmer 15-20 minutes, stirring occasionally. Pour over cooked spaghetti.

### Franks and Rice Chili

| | |
|---|---|
| 1 lb. frankfurters, cut 1" | 1/4 t. cumin |
| 1 onion, chopped | a few drops Tabasco |
| 2 T oil | 1 t. salt |
| 1 can each pinto and garbanzo | 1/2 t. ground mustard |
|    beans | 1 c. sour cream |
| 2 t. chili powder | |

Brown franks and onion lightly. Add rest of ingredients, except cream. Dissolve mustard in a tablespoon of water first. Simmer covered 15-20 minutes. Stir in cream and heat well without boiling. Serve over rice.

# Pork

### Basic Cooking

Cook pork slices 20 minutes (for 1/2" thick slice) to 45 minutes (1"). Allow 1 chop, or 3/8-1/2 pound of pork per person. Brown lightly in its own rendered fat or a little oil, then pan braise with an ounce or two of water, covered.

*With fruit:* Top with fruit slices or halves—pineapple, apple, peach, apricot, plum—while braising. Sprinkle with a bit of cinnamon and nutmeg.

*Apple sauce:* Cook covered with a pound of apple sauce, per four people. Sprinkle with caraway seed.

*Tomato and onions:* Top with slices of those vegetables and a sprinkling of basil, marjoram, or rosemary while braising.

### Stir-Fried Pork

Follow recipe for stir-fry beef (see p. 80), except use pork. Cut into bite sized pieces and cook 20 minutes in 2 T oil before continuing with vegetables

## Pork Stew

1 1/2 lbs. shoulder pork,
   cubed 1"
2 T oil
1 pt. spaghetti sauce
1 c. water
1/2 t. each, oregano and basil
1 t. salt

1/4 t. pepper
2 onions, quartered lengthwise, and leaves opened
1/2 lb. each, sliced zucchini
   and fresh beans, or frozen
4 carrots, julliened, or equivalent in frozen

Brown pork. Add rest except vegetables and bring to boil. Simmer covered 30 minutes. Add vegetables and simmer 20-30 minutes, until tender. If using frozen vegetables, add them at appropriate times according to package directions. Serve with potatoes.

## Sweet-Sour Pork*

1 1/2 lbs. pork, bite sized
2 T oil
2 T cornstarch
3 T soy sauce
1/2 c. water

1/4 c. sugar
3 T vinegar
1 cucumber and 1 onion,
   thinly sliced

Trim fat. Cook covered over low heat 20 minutes covered, or until cooked. Remove pork, sprinkle lightly with some of the soy and dredge in cornstarch. Brown pork over medium high flame. Add rest of soy and cornstarch, vinegar, water, and sugar to pan and mix well until dissolved. Cook over low heat until sauce is thickened and clear. Add pork and vegetables and heat until bubbly hot. Simmer 5 minutes. Keep vegetables crisp. Serve over rice.

## Chinese Pork Chops

4 pork chops
2 onions, sliced
1 clove garlic, minced
1 T oil
2 c. chicken bouillon
1/4 c. soy sauce
1/4 t. ground ginger

1 can bean sprouts, drained
1 can water chestnuts, drained
   and sliced
2 pkgs. frozen pea pods or cut
   beans
1 T cornstarch

Saute meat, onions and garlic about 5 minutes. Add half the bouillon, soy sauce, and ginger, and simmer covered 20 minutes.

Add rest of bouillon and vegetables, bring to boil and simmer covered according to time on vegetable directions. Add cornstarch dissolved in 1 tablespoon water and stir until thickened. Serve over rice.

## Pork Chops and Beans

| | |
|---|---|
| 4 pork chops | 1 1/2 t. salt |
| about 3 lbs. canned lima beans | 1/2 t. pepper |
| 1 T parsley flakes | 1/2 t. basil |

Trim chops and render fat. Brown chops and discard fat. Add rest, stir and bring to near boil. Simmer 30 minutes or until pork is done.

## Pork Chops with Rice

| | |
|---|---|
| 4 thick pork chops | 2 t. parsley flakes |
| 1 clove garlic, minced | 4 ribs celery, chopped |
| 4 c. chicken bouillon | 1 lg. onion, sliced |
| 2 c. rice (uncooked) | 2 tomatoes, sliced |
| 1 1/2 t. salt | 1 lg. green pepper, cored and |
| 1/4 t. pepper | sliced in thin rings |
| 1/4 t. sage or tarragon | |

Trim fat off chops. Render fat and remove pieces. Brown chops and garlic over medium flame. Pan braise chops 25 minutes, covered. Remove chops. Add bouillon, rice, and celery; stir well. Bring to boil. Lay chops on top, and then vegetables in turn. Cook for 20 minutes covered, or until rice is done. Do not stir after layering pork and vegetables.

## Pork Chops with Sour Sauce

| | |
|---|---|
| 4 pork chops | 1 t. paprika |
| 3/4 c. water | 1/2 t. caraway seed |
| 2 onions, sliced thin | 1/4 t. dill |
| sm. clove garlic, minced fine | 1 c. buttermilk or plain yogurt |
| 1 t. salt | |

Brown chops and drain fat. Mix rest into pan, except buttermilk. Simmer covered 3/4-1 hour or until chops are done. Remove chops and keep warm. Stir buttermilk into pan contents and heat well, stirring, but do not boil. Pour sauce over chops and cooked rice or noodles.

## Picnic Ham and Cabbage

2 lb. picnic ham approximate-
    ly, depending on fat and
    bone
8 potatoes, peeled or scrubbed

1 cabbage, cut in 4 quarters
1 t. caraway seed

Pinch the soft spots for fat when shopping for ham. Choose the leanest you can. Place whole in a 6 quart pot and cover with water. Bring to boil and simmer 1 hour, or time indicated on wrapper directions. Top with water if necessary. Add potatoes 20 minutes after start of simmer, and cabbage 20 minutes after that. Check potatoes to see if done, before ending cooking. If pot is too small, cook vegetables separately.

## Creamed Ham with Mushrooms*

1 lb. cooked ham slice, cubed
1 can cream of mushroom
    soup
8 oz. can mushrooms, drained

2 hard boiled eggs, diced
1/4 t. tarragon
8 stuffed olives, sliced

Heat soup over low flame. When hot add rest, stirring. Heat well and serve over noodles or as crepe filling. Substitute a white sauce for soup and a few fresh mushrooms cooking for one.

## Creamed Ham and Corn*

1 lb. cooked ham slice, cubed
1 can cream of chicken soup
3/4 c. milk
1 lb. canned corn kernels,
    drained

1 t. Worcestershire sauce
1 sm. onion, minced
1/2 t. ground mustard
1/2 t. salt
1/4 t. pepper

Mix all and simmer covered about 20 minutes. Serve over noodles, if desired. Substitute white sauce for soup and milk, when cooking for one.

## Ham and Noodles*

3/4 lb. ham slice, bacon,
    Spam, or Polish sausage,
    chopped

1 onion, diced
1 green pepper, chopped
2 T oil

1/2 t. marjoram or rosemary
1 lb. noodles, cooked al dente
2 eggs, beaten
1 c. plain yogurt

6 slices American or Swiss
   cheese, torn into bits
1 t. salt
1/4 t. pepper

If using bacon, precook and skip oil. Saute meat with onion, pepper, and spice until pepper is tender. Cook noodles separately, then add to meat mixture after draining. Toss and mix well. Keep pan on a low flame. Add rest of ingredients in turn, tossing. Serve when cheese is melted.

## Ham and Pasta Mix

3/4 lb. cooked ham slice,
   diced
1 T soy bacon bits
3 T oil
1 onion, chopped
4 stalks celery, chopped fine
8 oz. can mushroom pieces,
   drained
1 t. salt

1/4 t. pepper
1/8 t. nutmeg
1 lb. pkg. chariot wheels or
   any pasta with holes
1 c. cottage cheese
2 eggs, well beaten
1 c. buttermilk or sour cream
1/2 c. sharp cheese, grated
4 stuffed olives, sliced

Saute vegetables and condiments over medium flame in preheated pan until celery is almost tender to the bite. Add ham and bacon, and continue cooking for a few minutes. In your largest pot, cook pasta according to directions. Drain and replace in large pot. Keep off the stove. Add rest of ingredients, in turn, stirring briskly to coat pasta thoroughly. Mix in ham mixture and return for to stove on a very low flame, until the cheese melts in.

## Ham, Brussels Sprouts, and Cheese

1 lb. cooked ham slice, cubed
1 T oil
1 pkg. frozen brussels sprouts
   or broccoli
1 can cream of chicken or
   celery soup
1/2 can water

1/4 c. dry wine
4 oz. can mushrooms, drained
1/8 t. thyme
1/2 t. salt
1/4 t. pepper
6 slices American cheese, torn
   in strips

Brown ham slightly. Thaw vegetables by heating in a few teaspoons of water. Add to ham. Mix in rest, except cheese. Simmer covered 20 minutes. Make strips of cheese layered over top of mixture. Cover and continue simmering until cheese is melted. Spoon over noodles or rice.

## Ham with Rice*

| | |
|---|---|
| 2 chicken bouillon cubes | 2 8 oz. cans tomato sauce |
| 2 c. water | 1 T parsley flakes |
| 2 T oil | 1 t. salt |
| 2 onions, chopped | 1/4 t. pepper |
| 1 clove garlic, minced | 1/4 t. thyme |
| 1 green pepper, chopped | 1 bay leaf |
| 1 lb. ham slice, cubed 1/2" | 2 c. rice |

Boil water and dissolve bouillon. Set aside. Heat oil in pot and saute onions, green pepper, and garlic 5 minutes. Add rest, except bouillon and rice. Simmer covered 15 minutes. Stir occasionally. Add bouillon, bring to boil, and stir in rice. Simmer covered 20 minutes, or until rice is done. Uncover and simmer 5 minutes longer.

## Sausage, Basic Cooking

Jab each link with a fork (once is enough) to allow fat to escape and to keep them from bursting. Break up bulk meat or lay links in pan, adding about 1/4" boiling water. Cook over medium flame until water evaporates, then brown about 10 minutes on all sides. If you'll use the meat in a one-pot meal, just precook 5 minutes. Sausage will cook down, so allow about 50 percent more in your recipe than beef, about 1 1/2 lbs. for 4 people.

*Pork balls:* Pork version of meat balls, which can be used in spaghetti or any beef meat ball recipe. Mix 1 lb. bulk ground pork with 1 onion, chopped, 1 egg, 1/2 teaspoon salt, and 1/2 teaspoon paprika. Make into 1 1/2" balls and cook in boiling water 30 minutes. If to be used in spaghetti, precook them in water 10 minutes, drain and add to sauce for remainder of cooking. Bulk sausage can also be combined with beef or veal for other ground meat recipes.

*Italian sausage:* Use 1 lb. Slit lengthwise and saute about 15 minutes, draining fat. Substitute for ground meat in Meat Sauce for Spaghetti recipe.

*Pepperoni or chorizos:* Use 1 lb. Slice directly into spaghetti sauce and warm up.

## Sausage with Pasta

| | |
|---|---|
| 1 1/2 lbs. bulk pork sausage | 2 c. buttermilk |
| 1 green pepper, chopped | pinch cumin |
| 1 lg. onion, chopped coarsely | 2 t. chili powder |
| 2 c. tomato juice | 1/4 t. pepper |
| 1/4 t. basil | 3/4 lb. thin spaghetti, or el- |
| 1 t. salt | bow macaroni |
| 1 6 oz. can tomato paste | |

Precook sausage 5 minutes, breaking it up. Drain fat. Brown with onion and pepper. Stir in rest, except pasta. Bring to boil, then simmer uncovered 15 minutes. Cook pasta separately, al dente. Mix into sausage dish. Cook another 5 minutes, stirring.

## Polish Sausage and Beans

| | |
|---|---|
| 3 lbs. various canned beans, | 1/4 t. ground coriander |
|   drained—kidney, pinto, | pinch ground cumin |
|   lima, lentil, pork and beans | 1/2 t. ground mustard |
| 1 med. onion, chopped | 3/4 lb. Polish sausage |
| 1/4 c. dry wine |   (kielbasa), sliced 1/4" |
| 2 T sugar | |

Combine all ingredients except meat. Lay kielbasa slices on top. Heat over medium flame until near boiling, then simmer covered about 20 minutes.

## Polish Sausage and Sauerkraut in Beer

| | |
|---|---|
| 4 lg. potatoes, in jackets | 1 t. caraway seeds |
| 1 c. beer | 1 lb. Polish sausage or wurst, |
| 1 lb. can sauerkraut, drained |   cut in 4 equal parts |
| 1 onion, chopped | |

Scrub potatoes and boil until done, but still firm. Set aside. Mix all ingredients except sausage and potatoes in separate container. Place sausage in pan. Cover with sauerkraut mixture. Simmer covered about 15 minutes. Place potatoes on top and simmer another 10 minutes.

## Bigos (Polish Stew)

1 lb. sauerkraut
2 onions, chopped
2 T oil
3 oz. semi-sweet wine
8 oz. tomato puree
1 chicken bouillon cube
2 T flour
4 t. sugar
1 t. salt

1/4 t. pepper
1/2 t. cinnamon
1 bay leaf
1 lb. Polish sausage, cooked
   ham or Spam, cubed 1/2"
4 oz. can mushroom bits,
   drained
2 apples, diced

Place sauerkraut in colander; retain 2 oz. juice. Saute onion lightly. Combine sauerkraut juice, wine, tomato, bouillon, and flour. Cook until bouillon is dissolved and sauce somewhat thickened. Stir in sugar and condiments. Rinse sauerkraut well. Combine with pot contents and simmer covered 20 minutes or longer. Stir in meat, mushrooms, and apples, and simmer 15 minutes.

## Canadian Bacon and Beans

1 lb. Canadian bacon, cut in
   2" squares
2 T oil
1 t. salt
1 t. paprika

2 onions, chopped
1/2 t. marjoram
1 lb. cooked lentils or chick
   peas

Saute bacon and onions a few minutes. Add rest of ingredients and bring to boil. Simmer covered about 20 minutes. Stir occasionally. Take cover off for last 10 minutes to thicken.

## Pork and Lamb with Eggplant

3/4 lb. bulk pork sausage
3/4 lb. lamb, cubed 1/2"
1 c. beef bouillon
2 onions, chopped
1 lg. eggplant, cubed 1"
1 lb. potatoes, cubed 3/4"

1 pkg. cut beans, thawed
1 1/2 t. salt
1/4 t. pepper
1/2 t. oregano
1/4 t. basil

Cook sausage in 1 tablespoon water about 5 minutes, breaking meat up into chunks. Drain and add lamb, onions, and eggplant. Saute over medium low heat a few more minutes. Drain. Add rest of ingredients, bring to boil, and simmer covered 30 minutes. Serve over rice.

**Fried Rice with Pork**

6 c. cooked rice

2 eggs, scrambled semi-firmly

2 carrots, sliced 1/8"

1 onion, chopped

1 green pepper, diced 1/2"

1/2 lb. cooked pork

3 T butter

1/2 t. sugar

1/2 c. soy sauce

After cooking the first three ingredients, set them aside all in one container. Saute carrots in butter 10 minutes. Add rest of vegetables and saute until just before tender, 5 to 10 minutes. Dissolve sugar in soy. Chop up eggs with spatula. Combine all ingredients and cook over medium flame about 5 minutes, stirring rapidly. Shrimp, sauteed ground beef, or chicken may be used instead of pork. Cook shrimp at the same time as the onions and pepper.

# Marinade

Combine ingredients as follows. Place in secure plastic bag and let meat marinate at least 1 hour, preferably 2 or longer. This may be done conveniently between store and campground. In many recipes the marinade can be retained and added to stock in cooking. Marinade may also be made into a sauce or gravy.

*Beef:*

1 c. dry red wine, or vinegar

1 c. oil

1/2 t. salt

1/4 t. pepper

1/2 t. onion powder

pinch garlic powder

1 bay leaf

4 whole cloves

1/4 t. thyme

*Veal and Lamb:*

1/2 c. vermouth or sauterne

1/2 c. vinegar

1/2 c. oil

1 t. salt

1/4 t. pepper

1 t. onion powder

pinch garlic powder

pinch tarragon

1/4 t. rosemary

# Chicken

To cook chicken, place it in a pot large enough to hold all the pieces easily and cover well with water. Any extra broth you make can be used as liquid for the dish or in preparing rice.

Bring to a boil, lower the flame, and simmer (covered) from twenty to thirty-five minutes. Test with a fork. When the meat is to be used in a recipe and cooked longer, as in a curry, leave the meat somewhat on the firmer side.

With well-washed hands, strip meat from the bones. To handle the hot chicken place it into cold water for a few minutes, but don't let it soak; it'll lose juices. Better to break it apart roughly at first and let it air cool. By the time you strip the first piece, another will be manageable. For bite-sized pieces, you needn't cut the meat. Just tear with your fingers.

You needn't always pre-cook chicken; in some recipes, like "chicken with cream sauce," the meat is combined with the other ingredients at once, and cooked for a given time.

The fried chicken recipes here allow a whole breast (about a half pound or more of meat) per person. Cut that amount down when serving vegetables, rice, or breads on the side.

In recipes that call for boned chicken, it may be as cheap to buy it already boned rather than whole. You lose up to half of a whole chicken's weight in bone, gristle, skin, and fatty clumps. Compare the cost of whole versus boned. Economics aside, it takes time and is difficult to cut chicken off the bone.

## Fried Chicken*

2-3 breasts or equivalent
   chicken pieces
1" deep oil in skillet
1 egg, beaten

1/2 c. bread crumbs or flour
1 t. salt
1/4 t. pepper or 1/2 t. paprika

Rinse chicken. Leave skin on or off, as preferred. Preheat oil over medium flame. Coat pieces in egg and drop in plastic bag with crumbs and seasonings. Brown one side, about 5 minutes. Turn over, cover and cook on very low flame about 30 minutes, the last 5 uncovered over medium flame. Test with fork for tenderness. Any prepared, frozen vegetables, especially the ethnic kinds—Japanese, French—may be added to the same pot when chicken is almost cooked. Partially thaw 2 packages, add and cook as directed.

*Crisp-skin chicken:* Dip in buttermilk or yogurt before cooking.
*Wine:* Simmer in 1 cup dry wine instead of oil. Use 2 tablespoons oil for browning, then drain and add wine.
*Spices:* Add 1/2 teaspoon spice—rosemary, tarragon or thyme—to crumbs.
*Sweet curry:* Blend 1 cup any tart jam—plum, apricot, berry—with 1/2 cup dry wine in pan after browning. Mix in 2 teaspoons curry powder. Simmer as above. Baste chicken with sauce.
*Tomato-peanut butter sauce:* Combine 8 oz. can tomato sauce and 3 tablespoons peanut butter, heat and simmer chicken after browning.

## Stir-Fry Chicken

Follow recipe for stir-fry beef (see p. 80), except use 2 whole chicken breasts, boned and cut into 1" pieces. Cooking time should be about 10 minutes for the chicken. Skip the tomatoes and use any vegetables. You may add also about 1/4 pound cubed ham a few minutes before cooking is finished.

## Chicken Curry

2 boned chicken breasts
2 onions, chopped
1 clove garlic, minced
3 T oil

1 1/2 c. bouillon
1 c. tomato juice
1 1/2 T curry powder
1 t. salt

3 stalks celery, chopped
1/2 lb. sweet potato or yam,
  cubed 1"
1/4 c. flour dissolved in 1/4
  c. water
2 hardboiled eggs, chopped
  (optional)

2 apples, in chunks about 3/4"
2 bananas, sliced (optional)
handful of raisins
shredded coconut (optional)
peanuts

Saute chicken, celery, onion, and garlic. Add bouillon, tomato, curry, salt, and potato, and bring to boil. Simmer covered 20-30 minutes, until chicken just tender. Add rest, except peanuts and coconut. Simmer 5 minutes. Serve over rice; sprinkle with nuts.

### Spiced Chicken*

2 T lemon juice
1/4 t. ground cloves
1/2 t. cinnamon
1/4 t. pepper
1 t. salt
2 boned chicken breasts
3 T butter or oil

1 lg. onion, chopped
1 clove garlic, minced
1 t. sugar
6 oz. can tomato paste
1 pt. canned tomatoes
3/4 c. water
3 T flour

Mix first 5 ingredients in a plastic bag. Shake chicken in bag. Brown chicken on both sides. Remove chicken and saute onion and garlic. Add rest of ingredients, except chicken and flour. Simmer the sauce 1/2 hour, covered. Mix flour in a few ounces of cold water and add to sauce, along with the chicken. Simmer covered about 15 minutes if chicken boned, about 25 if whole sections. Serve with pasta and salad. Substitute 8 oz. tomato sauce for whole tomato and paste, if cooking for one person.

### Chicken with Rice I*

2 1/2-3 lbs. fryer, disjointed
2 T oil
3-4 stalks celery, chopped
1 green pepper, chopped
1 onion, chopped
2 c. rice

1 1/2 t. salt
1/4 t. pepper
6 stuffed olives, chopped
sm. jar pimentos, drained and
  chopped
1/2 c. sharp cheese, shredded

Boil chicken well, covered with water. Simmer until done, about 25 minutes. Remove from pot and let cool. Discard skin and remove meat from bones, tearing in bite sized pieces. In the meantime, saute celery, pepper, and onion about 5 minutes. Add 5 cups of the broth (add water if not enough broth), uncooked rice, salt and pepper. Cover, bring to boil and reduce heat. Simmer 20-25 minutes or until liquid is absorbed and rice is cooked. Add chicken and rest of ingredients and heat well, stirring thoroughly.

### Chicken with Rice II

2 T oil
2 1/2 lbs. chicken parts
1/4 lb. cooked ham, cubed
    1/2"
1/2 c. dry wine
1 lg. onion, sliced
2 tomatoes, roughly cut
1 green pepper, chopped

1/2 lb. zucchini, cubed 1"
6 black olives, minced
2 cloves garlic, minced
2 t. salt
1/4 t. pepper
1/2 t. oregano
2 1/2 c. chicken bouillon
1 1/2 c. rice, uncooked

Preheat oil and brown chicken well. Add rest of ingredients, except bouillon and rice. Turn down heat to very low and cook covered 20 minutes. Add water and rice, stir, and bring to boil. Simmer covered 20 minutes, or until rice is done.

### Chicken in Cream Sauce

2 1/2 lbs. frying chicken parts
2 onions, quartered lengthwise
    and separated
3 T butter
1 t. salt
1/4 t. pepper
1/2 c. dry wine

4 carrots, sliced 1/8"
2 tomatoes, chopped coarsely
1 c. coffee cream
4 ripe peaches, cut in 1/8s
2 T flour, dissolved in 2 T
    water

Use chicken with or without skin. Brown lightly with onions. Add wine and carrots, cover, and simmer 25 minutes. Add rest of ingredients, except flour. Simmer 15 minutes longer. Stir in flour and cook until thickened. Serve over pasta.

### Sour Cream Chicken

2 1/2 lbs. frying chicken parts
sm. clove garlic, minced
1 T oil
1 sm. onion, chopped fine

1/2 c. semi-sweet wine
1/2 t. salt
1/4 t. pepper
1/4 t. tarragon

1/4 c. water

1 pkg. frozen peas, thawed

1 c. sour cream, or plain yogurt

Brown chicken and garlic lightly over medium flame. Add onion, wine and seasonings. Simmer covered 15 minutes. Add water and peas and bring to boil. Simmer 15 more minutes. Set chicken aside. Stir in sour cream to make a sauce of the pan contents. Serve over chicken and cooked rice.

### Sweet-Sour Chicken

2 chicken breasts, boned and
cut bite sized

1 sm. egg, beaten

1/4 c. flour or bread crumbs

2 T oil

1 clove garlic, minced

1 t. salt

1/4 t. pepper

1 lb. can unsweetened pineapple chunks

12 oz. tomato juice

2 T vinegar

1 T sugar

1 t. ground ginger

2 green peppers, cored and
sliced

2 t. cornstarch, mixed in 1 T
water

Dip chicken in egg and roll in flour to coat well. Brown until golden. Mix in rest of ingredients, except green pepper and cornstarch, and bring to boil. Simmer covered 20 minutes. Add peppers and simmer 10 minutes longer. Stir in cornstarch and cook until thickened. Serve over plain rice.

### Chinese Chicken

2 1/2 lbs. frying chicken parts

1/2 t. ground ginger

1/4 t. pepper

1 lb. or more, frozen oriental
vegetables, green beans, or
pea pods, thawed

1 sm. onion

2 lg. tomatoes, cut in chunks

1/4 c. soy sauce

8 oz. can water chestnuts,
drained and sliced

3 T cornstarch, mixed in 4 T
water

handful of raisins and toasted
almonds

Cover chicken with water and bring to boil. Simmer 20 minutes. Leave 2 cups of broth in pot and set aside the rest to make rice. Strip and break up chicken into large sized pieces. Add ginger, pepper, vegetables, and soy, and bring to boil. Simmer covered until vegetables done, time according to package directions. Add cornstarch and simmer until sauce thickened, stirring. Make rice separately. Toss in raisins and almonds, fluffing it up. Serve chicken over rice.

### Chicken-Egg Foo Yung*

1 chicken breast, or 1/2 lb.
  canned chicken
3 ribs celery, finely chopped
1/4 c. oil
1 onion, finely chopped
1/2 t. ground ginger
8 eggs, well beaten

2 lbs. bean sprouts, drained
1 sm. can mushrooms, drained
  and chopped fine
3 T soy sauce
1 t. salt
1/4 t. pepper

If using raw chicken, cook until tender. Strip from bone and shred or chop fine. In fry pan, saute celery 3-4 minutes in half of the oil. Add onion, chicken, and ginger, and saute 3 minutes longer. Let cool somewhat and combine with sprouts, eggs, mushrooms, and condiments. Add rest of oil into the pan and heat well over medium flame. Drop large spoonfuls of the egg mixture into pan and fry golden brown on both sides. Serve with more soy if desired. If cooking for one person, substitute celery flakes and sprouts. Canned seafood may be used for chicken.

### Brunswick Stew

2 1/2 lbs. frying chicken
  pieces
1 lb. canned tomatoes, including juice
2 onions, quartered lengthwise
  and leaves opened
1 lg. potato, diced 1/2"

2 t. salt
1/4 t. pepper
1/4 t. poultry seasoning
1 pkg. each frozen lima beans
  and corn, thawed
2 T flour, dissolved in 1/4 c.
  water

Combine all ingredients except beans, corn and flour. Top with water to cover chicken, if necessary. Bring to boil, then simmer covered 15 minutes. Add lima beans and bring back to boil. Simmer 7 minutes. Add corn and bring back to boil. Simmer 3 minutes. Add flour and heat until stew thickens.

## Chicken Cacciatore

| | |
|---|---|
| 2 1/2 lbs. frying chicken pieces | 1/4 t. basil or thyme |
| 1 clove garlic, minced | 1 green pepper, chopped |
| 1 onion, chopped | 1/4 c. oil |
| 8 oz. can mushroom pieces, drained | 1 1/2 lbs. canned tomatoes |
| 1 t. salt | 1 t. oregano |
| 1/4 t. pepper | 1/2 c. dry wine |
| | 4 potatoes, quartered |
| | 1/4 c. grated Romano cheese |

Saute chicken, garlic, onion, and pepper until onion is limp. Add rest of ingredients, except potatoes and cheese. Simmer covered 15 minutes. Add potatoes. Top with water if necessary to almost cover. Simmer covered 20 minutes or until potatoes just tender. Uncover and simmer longer, until sauce thickens. Sprinkle with cheese a few minutes before taking off stove.

## Chicken Chop Suey*

Substitute chicken for ground beef in Ground Beef Chop Suey (see p. 96).

## Chicken and Banana*

| | |
|---|---|
| 2 T oil | 1/2 t. tarragon |
| 2 boned chicken breasts | 1/4 t. nutmeg |
| 1 med. onion, chopped | 1 t. salt |
| 4 slices orange, with peel | 1/4 t. pepper |
| 3/4 c. orange juice | 3-4 bananas, sliced |

Cut chicken into large bite sized pieces. Saute with onion and orange slices about 5 minutes over medium heat. Add rest except banana, cover and simmer 10-15 minutes. Add bananas and heat well. Serve with plain rice and spinach-avocado salad. Use 1 teaspoon orange peel and 1/4 cup water instead of orange for one person.

# Seafood

Fresh fish is bright colored, the gills red or pink on the inside, the eyes alive and globular. Once the colors fade, the gills darken and the eyes flatten out; look out. Press the flesh gently; it'll bounce back if fresh. Fresh fish should be kept just under freezing, which is impossible without it being enveloped in ice.

Check for dry-looking edges or off colors—whitish, yellowish, or any besides the natural fish pigmentation. In a frozen state, fish should be stored in ice. The store's thermometer should read no higher than $1^{o}F$ under any circumstances; the Bureau of Fisheries recommends $-5^{o}F$.

Fresh fish isn't available everywhere. If you're lucky enough to be in the Gulf Coast area of the United States, or any fishing port, you can buy it both fresh and relatively cheap. Otherwise, you can get frozen packages and let them thaw on the way to camp. Any fish that you buy is one of the easiest and fastest meats to cook. See the basic recipe for frying, for example.

Various cooked fish are available in cans too. They need only to be heated in the last few minutes of the recipe. Tuna is an emergency savior of many a day on the road. It can be found in the smallest store and has many uses. Two cans can substitute in almost any chicken recipe, or a can can be added to a salad or eaten in sandwiches with just a bit of yogurt or white sauce as a cream topping.

## Fried Fish*

| | |
|---|---|
| 1/4 c. milk | 1 1/2 lbs. fish fillets or steaks |
| 1 egg, beaten | 1 c. bread crumbs |
| 1 t. salt | 3 T oil |
| 1/4 t. pepper | |

Combine first 4 ingredients. Wash and pat dry the fish. Dip in the mixture and dredge with crumbs. Flour can be used instead if desired. Fry fish over medium heat 4-5 minutes each side. You should have a nice brown crust when through. A thick fish may take a minute or two longer. Test with a fork. Fish is done when it just flakes easily. Do not overcook. After frying, add 1/2 T parsley flakes and a few drops of lemon juice or vinegar into the pan. Heat it golden brown and pour over the fish as a sauce. Serve with tartar sauce.

## Fish Chowder

| | |
|---|---|
| 1 onion, chopped | 1/2 t. paprika |
| 3 ribs celery, chopped | 1 lb. fish, in large chunks |
| 2 T oil | 2-3 c. milk |
| 4 lg. potatoes, diced 1/2" | 4 slices American cheese, torn |
| 1 c. water | into bits |
| 1 t. salt | |

Saute onion and celery lightly. Add potatoes, water, and condiments. Bring to boil and simmer covered 10 minutes. Add fish. Top with a little water if necessary to almost cover the solids. Simmer covered 10 minutes. Stir in milk and cheese. Heat well until cheese melts completely, but do not boil. Cooked seafood may be substituted, in which case cook potatoes 20 minutes and add seafood with the milk.

## Creamed Shrimp

| | |
|---|---|
| 1 lb. shrimp meat | 1 t. salt |
| 2 T oil | 1/4 t. pepper |
| 1 T dried chives | 1/4 t. thyme |
| 4 oz. can mushrooms, drained | 1 1/2 c. sour cream |
| 1 1/2 T flour | |

In a preheated skillet or pan, combine oil and shrimp. At medium high flame, cook shrimp until it turns pink, no more than 5 minutes. Stir occasionally. Add mushrooms and cook until heated. Sprinkle the mixture with chives and then the rest, cooking two more minutes and stirring. Mix in sour cream. Take off the heat as soon as a boil is first reached. Serve over rice.

### Jambalaya

| | |
|---|---|
| 1 onion, chopped | 1 1/2 c. rice |
| 1 green pepper, chopped | 2 cans tomato soup |
| 1 clove garlic, minced | 2 cans of water |
| 2 T oil | 10 drops Tabasco |
| 1 t. salt | 1 lb. shrimp, after cleaning |
| 1 bay leaf | 1/2 lb. cooked ham, diced |
| 1/4 t. thyme | |

Saute vegetables a few minutes. Add liquids and condiments, stir and bring to boil. Sprinkle rice on top of mixture and pat down lightly under the surface. Cover and simmer 30 minutes. Add shrimp and ham and mix well. Simmer uncovered another 10 minutes. Browned ground beef may be used instead of shrimp and ham.

### Tuna Casserole

| | |
|---|---|
| 1 onion, chopped | 1/4 t. tarragon |
| 1/2 clove garlic, minced | 1 can cream of mushroom |
| 2 carrots, sliced 1/4" | soup |
| 1 green pepper, diced | 1 c. milk |
| 1/4 c. oil | 1 T lemon juice |
| 4 hard boiled eggs | 1 T flour |
| 1 t. salt | 1 can mushrooms, drained |
| 1/2 t. paprika | 2 7-oz. cans tuna |
| 1/2 t. mustard | 2 slices pimento, chopped |

Saute vegetables about 7 minutes, stirring over medium flame. Mash egg yolks in the same pan. Mix with soup and spices and heat. Add milk, blending it in well. Stir in lemon and flour dissolved in 2 T water. Cook until mixture is thickened. Mix in tuna, broken up, mushrooms, chopped egg whites, and pimento. Cover and simmer 15-20 minutes, or until carrots are tender. May be made with cooked chicken instead of tuna if desired.

### Tuna a la King

| | |
|---|---|
| 1 onion, chopped | 2 7-oz. cans tuna |
| 2 T oil | 1 lb. canned sugar peas, |
| 1 recipe white sauce |     drained |
| 1/2 t. ground mustard | 1 t. salt |
| 4 oz. mushroom pieces | 1/4 t. pepper |
| 2 t. lemon juice | |

Saute onion a few minutes. Make white sauce in the same pan with onion. Mix in rest of ingredients and bring to near boil. Serve over noodles.

### Tuna or Salmon Croquettes (from June Clifton)

| | |
|---|---|
| 2 7-oz. cans tuna or salmon | 1-2 c. wheat germ, or flour, |
| 2 onions, diced |     corn meal, cracker crumbs, |
| 2 lg. eggs |     or mixture |
| oil | |

Flake fish well, add onion, egg, seeds, and mix well. Add enough wheat germ to form a patty that holds together. Brown slowly in small amount of oil. Brown well on first side to insure that patty will hold together; turning it too soon may cause to break apart. Turn and brown on other side. Garnish with yogurt dressing (see "In the Raw" recipe, chapter 15), or melt cheese on top.

### Salmon Patties

| | |
|---|---|
| 1 basic recipe of rice, using | 1/4 c. grated cheese |
|     1/2 t. marjoram as spice | 1/2 c. bread crumbs |
| 1 lb. canned salmon | 1/4 c. oil |
| 4 eggs, beaten | 1 can tomato soup |
| 1 T lemon juice | |

Clean salmon of bone and skin, drain and break apart with fork. Beat together eggs, lemon and cheese. Combine rice and salmon, and then stir in egg mixture. Make into patties and dredge with crumbs. The patties will be somewhat fragile so handle gingerly. (Your hands will be sticky by now, so have a helper ready to pour warm water over your hands so you can wash.) Fry patties about

4 minutes on each side over medium flame in preheated pan—a little longer if you like a crisp skin. Warm the tomato soup and pour over patties, to taste, when serving.

*Potato variation:* Boil 6 fairly large potatoes, quartered, and mash with 3 tablespoons butter, 1 teaspoon salt and 1/3 cup milk or buttermilk. Substitute for rice, reducing eggs to 2 and skipping bread crumbs. (But add the onion and marjoram, which would have been in rice.) Fry as above.

*With ham:* Use minced ham or corned beef instead of salmon in potato variation. Add 1/2 teaspoon mustard instead of marjoram.

### Crab Cakes*

| | |
|---|---|
| 1 lb. crab, after cleaning | 1/2 c. bread crumbs |
| 2 eggs, beaten | 1 t. Worcestershire sauce |
| 2 oz. milk | 1/2 t. salt |
| 2 T parsley flakes | 1/4 t. pepper |
| 1 sm. onion, finely chopped | 3 T oil |

Chop crab finely. Let parsley soak in milk a few minutes to reconstitute. Combine all ingredients and shape into cakes. Fry over medium flame until browned on both sides. Serve with tartar sauce, salad, and hush puppies. Use a small can crab meat for one person.

### She-Crab Soup (from John Liberatos, Charleston, South Carolina)

| | |
|---|---|
| 1 c. white crab meat | 3 ribs celery, chopped fine |
| 1/8 c. crab roe | 2 c. milk |
| 2 T butter | 1/2 c. cream |
| 1 T instant minced onion | 2 T Worcestershire sauce |
| 1/4 t. salt | 2 t. flour |
| 1/8 t. pepper | 1 T water |
| 1/2 t. mace | 3 T sherry |

Place first 8 ingredients in double boiler and simmer 5 minutes. Heat milk and add, stirring, then cream and Worcestershire. Thicken with flour dissolved in 1 tablespoon water. Add sherry. Cook over very low heat 1/2 hour. Can be made without roe. Shrimp may be substituted.

## Sardine Sandwiches

| | |
|---|---|
| 1-2 sticks butter | bread |
| 3 cans sardines, about 10-12 oz. | 1 lb. shredded cheese |
| | mustard |
| 1 green pepper, diced | |

Saute pepper in some of the butter until tender. Take pan off fire and remove pepper temporarily. Butter slices of bread on one side. Place a few in frying pan, buttered side down. Layer bread lightly with cheese, green pepper, sardines split in half, and more cheese. Add mustard and some salt and pepper, if you wish. Place slices of bread on top, buttered side up. Toast sandwiches on medium high flame. When first side is browned, turn over. Cover partially to help melt cheese.

## Clam Chowder

| | |
|---|---|
| 3 doz. clams in the shell, or about 1 lb. canned (keep juice) | 1/2 bay leaf |
| | 4 potatoes, diced |
| | 1 tomato, chopped small |
| 2 onions, chopped fine | 1 T parsley flakes |
| 3 ribs celery, chopped fine | 1 pt. water |
| half stick butter, or 1/4 c. oil | 1 t. salt |
| 1/2 t. pepper | 1 qt. milk, or 1 pt. each milk |
| 1/4 t. thyme | and coffee cream |

Steam clams in the shell 10 minutes, until they open. Remove and chop meat and set aside. (Or use canned clams, undrained. Keep those aside also.) Saute onions and celery about 5 minutes in some of the butter. Or render a cube of salt pork, if you can get it, and saute in that. Throw out the pork. Add tomato, potatoes, parsley, and water, and bring to boil. Simmer covered 20 minutes, or until potatoes are cooked. Add condiments and milk and simmer on very low heat 10 minutes longer. Stir in clams and heat well.

## Shrimp Creole

| | |
|---|---|
| 1 1/2 lbs. shrimp | 2 onions, chopped |
| 1 clove garlic, minced | 1 1/2-2 lbs. canned tomato |
| 3 stalks celery, chopped | 1 1/2 t. salt |
| 1 green pepper, chopped | 1 t. paprika |
| 2 T butter or oil | 1/2 t. basil |

1/2 t. thyme                              1 bay leaf
1 T parsley flakes                        few drops Tabasco

Cook shrimp in boiling salted water about 8 minutes. Cool, peel, and devein. Saute celery, garlic, and pepper about 5 minutes. Add onion and saute another 5 minutes. Chop up tomatoes and add with other ingredients. Cover and let simmer about 20 minutes. Stir in shrimp and rewarm a few minutes. Serve over rice.

# Bread and Eggs

"Anything you can eat for supper, you can eat for breakfast," Maureen used to say when she saved her leftovers for the next morning.

It's certainly true that the stomach doesn't know the difference. It dutifully breaks everything down into simpler elements. Most of our breakfast habits are a consequence of tradition. Our "hearty" morning starter of bacon, eggs, and pancakes is incomprehensible to the European. He eats a customary scone, or bread with jam and soft cheese, and a piece of fruit.

An older and more tender constitution than Maureen's—she was seventeen at the time of our trip—may turn slightly squeamish at the thought of last night's beef stew being tossed around during the morning ride. It may prefer things blander, more easily digestible, in the morning. Traditionally, those have been cereals and eggs.

Cereals are the staff of life in much of the world because meats are either unavailable or too expensive. The mass of people must eat the cheaper and universal grains. Cereals are essential for a bicyclist, or any active road traveler, to satisfy his or her voracious appetite. Along with sugars, they're the "coal" that's constantly stoked into a seemingly bottomless furnace.

Most people think of cornflakes or other dry, ready-to-eat products when cereal is mentioned. That may be convenient, but these require fresh milk, unless the taste of powdered milk is agreeable.

I like hot cereals because you can eat them without milk. I've even learned to prefer them that way, using instead raisins, spice, and bits of fruit to add variety and as partial substitutes for sugar. Hot cereals are all jiffy types now, needing only a minute of cooking.

There are other cereals in the grain family, of course. Bread is the most basic, so much so that the word is synonymous with food the world over—"Give us this day our daily bread"—and each culture has its characteristic version: Mexican tortillas, Indian chapatis, Jewish rye, corn cakes from the southern United States, black Russian bread, Middle East Pita.

As extenders, prepared breads are handled and eaten in the simplest ways: dipped into gravy, used to hold food as a tortilla, or buttered and fried in a pan as with corn muffins or toasted cheese sandwiches. An oven of some sort is needed to make these true breads. Since our kind of traveler has no room for one, I list no recipes for baking bread. But you may enjoy the "quick-breads"—those using fast-acting leavening and made on top of the stove—that I have included. Unless otherwise specified, general purpose flour, either bleached or unbleached, is meant in these recipes.

A note on baking powder: it's not the same as baking soda and the two shouldn't be interchanged. Soda is used to counteract the acidity in recipes that contain buttermilk, yogurt, vinegar, and other acidic liquids. Baking powder is usually added to those too.

Fried breads are popular in America. Hoe cakes, hush puppies, fritters, and French toast need only a frying pan. Some call for frying in a volume of oil. They can be made at a time when you're replenishing the oil supply. A full bottle of oil is a problem to carry and the amount can be cut down by making one of those recipes.

Dumplings can be placed in the pot on top of a stew, any meat dish, or beans, and allowed to cook for the last ten minutes of preparation—so can commercially packaged biscuit rolls.

Making pancakes takes special care. The secret of light ones is to not overmix the batter and not overcook the cake. Mix all dry ingredients together with a fork or whisk, using the tossing motion described on page 44 to approximate sifting. Work part of the flour mixture well into the egg or other liquid and make a thick paste. Blend in oil and then the rest of the liquids. Now add the rest of the flour mixture. Mix thoroughly, but don't beat the batter. Leave lumps; they'll disappear in baking, and your cakes will be lighter from the air trapped in them. If the batter is either too thin or thick, add more flour or liquid. It should flow, but not run. The thicker the batter, the thicker the cake.

Preheat the pan over a medium flame. Test the pan with a few drops of water; they should sputter and bounce around. Unless you are using a pan with a non-stick surface, grease the pan with a few drops of oil. Pour batter in a small pool to make cakes about six inches in diameter. You can add pieces of fruit—berries, apples, peaches—to the surface of the cake at this time if you wish. Push them in gently and dribble some batter on top of each piece.

Turn the pancake when its edges start drying and bubbles appear on the surface, in about three minutes. Peek underneath first to see if it is brown. Don't continue baking until the bubbles break; your pancakes will lose air and become heavy. Brown the other side a couple of minutes. Serve with breakfast meats or eggs and top with syrup, honey, or a topping of your choice.

With thicker batter the heat should be lowered slightly to cook thoroughly. After preheating, turn down the flame to medium low and brown well to cook the cake through.

Crepes are somewhere between pancakes and omelets and are no harder to make. The batter is blended well to remove lumps, however, and is mixed much thinner. Cooking takes just a minute or so for each side, over a medium flame. Crepes can be eaten by themselves, as a complete meal—lots of protein with all those eggs—or they can be filled with any number of creamed meats, vegetables, or with jams for a dessert.

For special occasions, you might surprise your group with crepes suzette. This calls for brandy being set on fire. The burst of flame at the climax of preparation will certainly raise eyebrows —but be careful not to singe any of them.

Eggs are ubiquitous. No part of the world is without them, even if chickens aren't ordinarily on menus.

One would think that, being so widespread, eggs would be foolproof. Yet they're probably the most commonly ill-prepared dish of all. Witness the thousands of diners across American in which a breakfast request for "over light" turns out like peanut brittle, and "well-done" has to be cut with a sharp knife. It's the same in the rest of the world: in Pakistan, for example, the word "omelet" is synonomous with our "sunny side up," and the yolk is cooked solid.

Since the beginners I've met on the road hadn't the slightest notion of how to begin, I include all the ways one can cook eggs in a pan, no matter how simple. Contrary to the usual presentation, however, I start with the most difficult technique, omelet making, and work down to the easiest. Once you can make an omelet well, you can make any of the others.

These dishes are primarily intended for breakfast, but they can easily be part of main meals. Omelets in particular can be filled with various creamed meats, fish, and vegetables, or with cream sauces.

All egg techniques depend on low heat to keep them from getting tough—another reason to have a stove with a good simmering control. Salt is widely thought to toughen eggs too, if added before the cooking process. I don't notice it myself but you might wait until the eggs are almost done before salting, if you think it's a significant factor in their texture. Spices, on the other hand, should be beaten in with the eggs; their flavor will be released more thoroughly when heated.

# Bread

### Oatmeal with Spices*

4 c. water
1 t. cinnamon
1/2 t. nutmeg
handful of raisins
1 t. salt

2 c. quick oatmeal
1 T butter
sliced fruit—banana, peach or
    ripe pear

Bring to boil first 4 ingredients. Stir in salt and oats. Lower flame, bring to a low boil and cook 1 minute, stirring. Add butter and fruit and stir. Let stand a few minutes before eating. Sugar or honey and milk may be added. Cream of wheat also goes well with these spices. Just change the proportions of cereal to water, according to package instructions.

## French Toast*

3 eggs, beaten                    12 or more slices bread
1/2 t. salt                       oil
2 c. milk

Preheat lightly oiled pan over medium flame. Combine eggs, salt, and milk. Dip bread on both sides in the mixture. Don't soak the bread. Brown both sides. Add a few drops of oil when needed. Top with any sweet sauce, syrup, or cinnamon-sugar mix.

## Pancakes (from June Clifton)

2 c. buckwheat or whole          3 T baking powder
   wheat flour                   1 t. sea salt
1 c. of any: wheat germ, oats,   2 eggs, beaten
   corn meal, raisins, sesame    seasonings, according to taste
   seeds, fresh or leftover vege-  2 c. milk, or yogurt
   tables or rice, chopped       4 T oil
   apple, cottage cheese, tuna,  1 T honey (optional)
   cereal, spinach, mashed
   bananas, more flour, or a
   mixture

Combine flour, baking powder, and seasonings (for example, a pinch of nutmeg with cottage cheese or apple). Add the ingredient(s) of your choice from the group above. Mix well. Add milk, honey, eggs, and oil; stir only until all ingredients are moist. Lumpy batter is fine; pour about 1/4 cup onto fairly hot skillet for each pancake. When bubbles form on top, turn over. Turn only once. Serve at breakfast or as a main course at dinner, depending on ingredients.

## Griddle Cakes (from June Clifton)

1 c. cornmeal                    1/2 t. salt
3/4 c. of any: oats, flour, left-  1 1/2 t. baking powder
   over rice, kasha or potatoes,  3 T oil
   or more cornmeal, or a        1 egg
   mixture                       about 1 c. milk
1 T honey (or diced onion and
   green pepper)

Combine all ingredients. Drop by 1/4 cup onto oiled and pre-heated skillet. Brown both sides. Serve for breakfast or as cornbread.

**Sweet Milk Pancakes**

| | |
|---|---|
| 2 1/2 c. flour | 3 eggs, lightly beaten |
| 1 T baking powder | 2 c. milk |
| 1 t. salt | 5 t. oil or melted butter |
| 1 T sugar | |

Toss together dry ingredients. Stir into the liquids. Bake as described in the introduction to breads. For lighter cakes, separate eggs; mix yolks with some flour, milk, and oil, then rest of flour. Fold in stiffly beaten whites into the batter.

*Wheatcakes:* Use 1 1/4 cups each of whole wheat flour and general purpose flour in sweet milk recipe. Add sliced fruit for variety.

**Buttermilk Pancakes**

| | |
|---|---|
| 2 c. flour | 2 T honey or sugar |
| 1 t. baking soda | 2 eggs, lightly beaten |
| 1 t. baking powder | 1/2 stick butter or 4 T oil |
| 1 t. salt | 2 c. buttermilk |

Combine dry ingredients and continue as described in Introduction.

*Cornmeal pancakes:* Substitute 1 1/2 cup cornmeal and 1/2 cup flour for 2 cups flour in buttermilk pancakes. These cakes are very filling.

*Buckwheat cakes:* Substitute 1 1/2 cups buckwheat flour and 1/2 cup flour for 2 cups flour in buttermilk pancakes. Also increase buttermilk to 3 cups and decrease oil to 2 tablespoons.

**Crepes***

| | |
|---|---|
| 2 c. flour | 1 T sugar (optional) |
| 1 1/2 t. baking powder | 6 eggs, beaten well |
| 1 1/2 t. salt | 2 c. milk |
| 1 1/2 t. grated lemon rind | 1 c. water |
| (optional) | 3 T melted butter or oil |

Mix the dry and liquid ingredients separately. Add dry to liquid gradually. Work out lumps but don't overbeat. Bake in ungreased non-stick pan over medium flame, or use a few drops of oil in regular pan. Brown lightly both sides. Top with any sweet sauce, jam, or honey and roll up or use to make blintzes. Crepes may be filled with various creamed mixtures—fish, meat, or eggs—to prepare as a main dish.

*Crepes suzette:* Instead of lemon in crepes batter, use 2 teaspoons brandy or cognac. Bake crepes and keep warm. Spread the crepes sauce, below, on each crepe. Roll and place on preheated large platter or individual plates. Cover crepes with about a quarter inch of warmed brandy or liqueur. Light and let burn down. For extra sweetness, sprinkle a little sugar over the crepes before lighting them. The flame will make caramel of the sugar. Spoon leftover sauce over the crepes.

*Crepes sauce:* Combine 1/4 cup melted butter, 1 cup honey, 1/2 cup orange juice, 4 teaspoons lemon juice and 2 teaspoons grated orange rind.

## Nalesniki (Polish Crepes)*

| | |
|---|---|
| 3 c. flour | 1 1/2 c. milk |
| 1 1/2 t. baking powder | 1 1/2 c. water |
| 1 T sugar | 1 1/2 T oil |
| 1/4 t. salt | any sweet sauce |
| 6 eggs, separated | |

Combine ingredients, mix, and bake as described for milk pancakes. Bake a 7-10" cake. When underside is lightly browned, about 4 minutes, turn over and fry other side only 30-45 seconds. If insides are not done, turn down flame and bake somewhat longer on the first side. Serve on plate light side up, cover with sauce and roll up.

## Blintzes

| | |
|---|---|
| 1 recipe of crepes | 2 t. sugar |
| 8 oz. creamed cottage cheese | 1/2 t. salt |
| 4 oz. cream cheese, warmed | 1/2 t. cinnamon |
| 1 egg, beaten | 3 T butter |

Make crepes and keep warm. Place about 1 1/2 tablespoons of the above ingredients, combined well, into the center of each crepe. Fold corners over to make a kind of envelope. Brown on both sides over medium flame. Top with sour cream or a sweet sauce.

## Fritters

2 c. flour
1 t. baking powder
1 t. baking soda
1/4 c. sugar
1/2 t. salt
1/2 t. nutmeg

1 1/2 c. buttermilk
2 eggs, beaten
1/3 c. oil, or to cover pan 1/4"
10 med. apples, sliced 1/4"

Combine dry ingredients, tossing with a fork. Beat well with milk, and then eggs. Dip apples in the batter and fry in oil preheated well over a low flame, about 3 minutes on each side. Cooked corn, blueberries, sliced bananas, raisins, or drained, crushed pineapple may be mixed into the batter also, dropped by spoonfuls into the pan and fried likewise. Sprinkle with sugar or syrup.

## Hush Puppies

2 c. cornmeal
1 T flour
1 t. salt
1 1/2 t. baking powder
1 sm. onion, chopped

1 egg, well beaten
1 c. milk
1/2 c. water
few drops Tabasco
oil, about 1/2" in pan

Combine first 4 ingredients. Mix into the egg and liquids, and add onion. Blend well. Preheat oil over medium to high flame. Drop batter by the tablespoonful and let cook until brown. Turn as it cooks. Hush puppies are a good way to use leftover oil.

## Hoe Cakes*

2 c. cornmeal
1 T baking powder
2 t. sugar
1 t. salt

8 T oil
2 1/2 c. boiling water
oil, about 1/8" in pan

Combine first 4 ingredients. Mix in gradually 8 tablespoons oil. Pour in boiling water and stir to make a kind of dough. It'll be more like heavy wet sand than bread dough. Shape into flat cakes. (Your hands will be oily so be ready with some tissue to wipe them between sessions at the pan.) Preheat pan over moderate to high flame and cook until golden brown, about 3-4 minutes on each side. Watch how you put them in: they'll sizzle.

## Dumplings

| | |
|---|---|
| 1 1/2 c. flour | 1/2 c. milk |
| 2 t. baking powder | 2 t. oil |
| 1/4 t. salt | 1 lg. egg, beaten |
| 1/4 t. rosemary or cumin | |

Combine dry ingredients. Add a little of each of the liquids gradually to flour mixture, making a dough. Stir only long enough to make all dry ingredients moist; don't beat. Drop spoonfuls into boiling soups, stews, or chili. If batter is too thick to drop off readily, thin it with some milk. Cover and simmer 10-12 minutes. Don't fill the pot to the top. These dumplings will expand and may push off the cover. Also avoid opening the cover and letting out the steam.

## Chapati* (from Anadi Naik, Cuttack, India)

This simple quick bread is common in India, where it serves as both a utensil—food is picked up with the hands using the chapati to pinch it—and a foil for the spicy foods of that country. To make, add water to about 2 to 3 cups of brown or regular flour, a pinch of salt and 1 tablespoon oil. Knead the dough into a stiff paste. Form a round ball an inch in diameter, press it with your palms to make it flat and roll it out about 1/4" or thinner. Fry a few minutes on each side in light oil. Don't make chapatis with bland foods; they have no taste. Serve instead with curries and chilis, like a Mexican tortilla.

# Eggs

## Basic Omelet*

| | |
|---|---|
| 2-3 eggs per person | 1/8 t. salt per egg |
| 1 t. butter or oil per egg | 1/8 t. pepper per 2 eggs |
| 1 T milk or water per egg | |

Preheat the skillet well over low flame. Add butter or oil, tilting skillet to grease its sides. Use half or less oil, or omit, with a non-stick pan. Beat egg mixture well and pour into pan. Complete cooking should take 6-10 minutes, depending on heat and pan. Flow or move bits of uncooked egg to the sides with the edge of the spatula. Lift edges to let uncooked egg flow underneath for even cooking. When eggs are just set (but still wet looking) work the edges of the omelet loose on one side and fold over. Fry the omelet for about 30 seconds longer to seal edges. Don't make over 6 eggs in an 8-10 inch pan. Better to make two batches. Cheese or various cream sauces and creamed meats can be folded in or poured over an omelet for a main meal.

## Omelet Variations*

*Cheese:* When omelet is half done, add strips of American or other cheese on one half. Fold over onto that half. Keep in pan another minute or so to melt cheese.

*Mushroom, tomato, onion or green pepper, chopped:* Add sauteed bits, about a handful per pan, before folding over.

*Ham, sausage or bacon:* Sprinkle chopped bits before folding. You can use imitation soy bacon too.

*Condiments:* Add 1 teaspoon instant parsley or chives per egg to mixture before cooking. Use other seasonings (about 1/8 teaspoon per egg)—curry, nutmeg, chervil, basil, dill, marjoram, saffron (if you can afford it), oregano, tarragon, chili powder, or thyme.

*Jams and jellies:* For those with a yen for additional sugar, spread 1 teaspoon per egg before folding.

*Vegetables:* Most vegetables, first boiled and then sauteed and creamed in white sauce, can be poured over or inserted in an omelet. Leave some cooked vegetables from supper for the morning.

## Fluffy Omelet*

The basic omelet, with slight differences: separate the eggs. Beat well all ingredients with the yolks. About 1/4 teaspoon baking powder per egg can be added to make the omelet fluffier. Beat whites stiff. Fold the yolk mixture into whites. Pour into pan, cover, and cook over a very low flame. When the bottom is slightly brown, cut through the middle and fold over carefully.

## Mixed Omelet

| | |
|---|---|
| 1 onion, chopped | 1/4 lb. minced meat (canned |
| 1 green pepper, chopped | or deli counter, or soy |
| 1/4 c. oil | bacon bits) |

8 eggs, well beaten
1 t. salt
1/4 t. pepper
1/2 t. oregano
4 oz. can mushrooms,
　chopped

1/8 t. basil
6 slices American cheese, torn
　in strips

Use a 10" skillet or a large, heavy duty pan. Saute onions and pepper about 4-6 minutes, using half of the oil. Stir in meat and saute lightly. Separately, mix rest of ingredients except cheese. Add rest of oil to pan. Pour the egg mixture into the pan and let cook over very low heat. Pick up corners to let liquid run to the bottom. Cover partially to retain heat and help set the eggs. When top is no longer fluid, place cheese on surface. Simmer until cheese melts.

## Poached Eggs

I've never known an active traveler who was concerned enough about the fat used in making eggs to ask for poached eggs. Still . . . . gently slip the desired number of cracked eggs (no more than 6 at a time; don't crowd) into salted water that has just reached a boil. Lower heat, cover pan, and let simmer about 4 minutes or until the whites are firm. For more eggs, you might try a tricky technique in a large pan of water. Stir the boiling water with a long wooden spoon to make a circular whirlpool. Drop the cracked eggs easily into its middle. Cover pan and let cook. The eggs will stay more or less in a mass. Probably more mess than mass: I know no one who's proficient in this. The only foolproof method is with a set of egg poachers (small aluminum cups to hold eggs). Save yourself the trouble of carrying those; fry or boil eggs instead.

## Scrambled Eggs*

Ingredients as in basic omelet, but milk or water may be omitted. Follow same preparations, in general, but stir egg mixture often with spatula or fork, lifting bits of cooked portions from the bottom and bringing them to the top. Frying will usually take less time than an omelet, but a large number of eggs may take up to 15 minutes on a low flame.

*Variations:* Add any of the spices listed for omelets. With meats, mushroom, onion, and green pepper, saute first in butter before adding egg mixture. Scrambled eggs also combine well with creamed dishes and cheese. A neat technique is to butter slices of bread and place them butter side down in the pan, after lifting out temporarily the scrambled eggs. Cover the bread with slices of American cheese and then with the eggs. Toast over a medium flame about 3 minutes or until the bread is browned.

### Fried Eggs*

Preheat pan well, grease, and break eggs into it carefully so as not to break the yolks. "Tease" the whites in portions where they show clear to make them run to edges and be cooked. Cooking will only take a few minutes, depending on heat. Turn eggs over gently and cook other side a minute or so if desired. Don't fry more than 6 eggs at a time in a pan. Fry meats separately first.

### Boiled Eggs*

Certainly the easiest. Cover eggs with water, but don't pile them one on the other. Bring to boil and simmer for desired time: up to 5 minutes for soft, as much as a half hour for really hard, about 12 minutes on the average. Cool them 1 minute in water immediately to stop cooking and to help prevent the yolk from turning dark. To keep eggs from cracking while being cooked, make a small hole in the large end with a safety pin or a knife point. Using eggs which are at room temperature helps too.

### Mexican Ranch Eggs

| | |
|---|---|
| 1 onion, chopped | 2 T oil |
| 1 green pepper, diced | 2 8-oz. cans tomato sauce |
| 1 clove garlic, minced | 1 tomato, chopped |
| 6 drops Tabasco | 1/2 t. each, basil and oregano |
| 1 t. salt | 8 eggs |

Saute onion, pepper, and garlic until pepper is almost tender. Add rest of ingredients except eggs, and bring to boil. Simmer covered 15 minutes. Break eggs very carefully over sauce and place separately in sauce. Cover and simmer 5 minutes longer, or until eggs are poached. Serve over muffins, coarse bread, or tortillas.

## Creamed Eggs*

1 c. white sauce recipe (see
  p. 158)
8 hard boiled eggs, chopped
1 T lemon juice
1/8 t. nutmeg

1/2 stick butter
1 dozen English muffins
6 slices boiled ham
12 slices of tomato

Combine white sauce with eggs, lemon, and nutmeg. Cut ham slices into halves and fry slightly. Slice muffins in half. Butter the cut sides and toast in pan over medium flame, buttered sides down. Turn muffins over and layer 12 of the halves with ham, tomato, and egg mixture. Cover with the other halves and re-warm. You'll be able to re-warm only a few at a time, even in a large pan. Instead of meat, you may use cooked broccoli, spinach, cut beans, peas, or cut-up asparagus.

# Traveling Without Meat

The main courses and soups in this chapter are all meatless. Nutritional requirements—proteins, carbohydrates, vitamins, minerals—are met by the natural state of their ingredients: the grains, vegetables, eggs, and cheeses. Nothing is added to or taken from the original goodness of those elements.

Grains, and their pasta forms, are also the original dehydrated foods. You can't find more concentrated, easily carried and measured foods and considerably cheaper than freeze dried. This makes them a double boon in road cooking.

Like the breads, rice is common throughout the world. From Spain to Sumatra you'll find it used as the basis of famed dishes. It's one of the most amenable of ingredients, graciously deferring to the taste of an added sauce or spice, but without losing its own texture and character. A Near East pilau is a lightyear away from rice pudding in taste, yet you're aware that you're eating rice in both dishes.

Use regular rice rather than the instant type—instant feels dry to the taste. It's also more expensive by about fifty percent. In America the choices are among short or long grained, white, or brown rice. Overseas, you may find only one kind in many areas.

Pastas are robust and economical fillers. They are easily prepared, either separately or in combination with other ingredients. A biker rides well on these carbohydrates.

Until I was about thirteen, I never knew about fresh pasta. My

137

mother always bought the canned kind of spaghetti, awful stuff in a sugared tomato sauce that bore almost no trace of that vegetable's taste. For all those years I thought that's how spaghetti came—grown soggy in the ground in those short spongy pieces and then canned like worms.

My first spaghetti at the home of an Italian friend was a revelation. Was this the same dish? I couldn't believe it. I've never had it from a can again, but people tell me it still tastes the same as I remember it from childhood.

It therefore astonishes me that pasta is still actually cooked in huge factory vats and canned, to soak for months, perhaps years. More amazing yet is that anyone would buy it, either in that form or freeze dried. After all, it takes hardly more effort to make pasta than it does to open and heat the canned kind. The worst of it is that some camping authors recommend canned spaghetti for its convenience. What foolishness!

"If you're John's assistant, start chopping onions or garlic first thing—whatever the menu, you'll need them for sure with him as cook." That's what the other bikers usually say about me on trips, and it's true that I like them with a passion.

The onion is reputed to clean the blood, protect against viral diseases, and aid in problems with blood clots. According to studies reported in *Prevention* magazine, garlic acts against bacteria responsible for stomach disorders. It's also supposed to help prevent heart attacks, lower cholesterol levels, and inhibit growth of tumor cells. A garlic extract in a spray will kill five species of mosquito. Mediterranean peasants wear garlands of garlic around their necks to ward off colds and evil spirits.

Dogs seem to sense intuitively the amazing powers of these foods. My dogs seek out and chew wild onion in the lawn. With all these testimonials, how can I resist liking them? But they're only one of the vegetables I enjoy. Vegetables are naturally nutritious and relatively cheap, and they simply taste good. They deserve a prominent place in your kitchen.

The lowly potato requires special mention; it's the clumsy clod of the carbohydrates. The potato's aristocratic Italian cousins, the pastas, are willowy and of high delicate color. Rice is light and dainty. But the potato is heavy, covered with pock marks and dark skinned.

In spite of their peasant cast, potatoes have been the dependable crop for centuries along a broad band through northern Europe. Poor potato crops caused famines in Ireland and Germany.

They can likewise be a mainstay for travelers. They're readily available at all times of the year, in areas where rice is not, and they fill stomachs well. Except for the fact that they can't be carried easily from day to day, potatoes are a good choice for your cooking pot.

**Most of the recipes in this chapter are from June Clifton.**

### Split Pea Soup*

5 c. boiling water or stock
1 1/2 c. dry split peas
1 onion, chopped
1 bay leaf
1 T celery seed
1 t. cumin

2 ribs celery, chopped (optional)
2 T oil (optional)
sprouts, parsley or grated cheese

Pour split peas slowly into boiling stock so as not to stop boiling. Once stock has resumed its brisk boil, cover pan with tight lid, and simmer peas 30-40 minutes until soft. Remove from heat and beat to make as smooth as possible. Add chopped onion. For tastier soup, saute onion and celery in oil, then add to soup. If soup seems too thick, add water or milk to get desired consistency. Stir in seasonings. Simmer a few minutes. Then let soup steep for about 5 minutes. Keep pot covered tightly. Garnish with grated cheese, parsley, sprouts or anything else you desire.

### Lima Bean Soup*

5 c. boiling water or stock
1 1/2 c. dry lima beans
1 T celery seed
1 T cumin
1 T garlic powder
pinch of cayenne
1 lg. onion, chopped

1 bay leaf
2 ribs celery, chopped (optional)
2 carrots, chopped (optional)
2 T oil (optional)
grated cheese or yogurt

To cook, follow recipe for Split Pea Soup except don't beat.

## Lentil Soup*

4 c. boiling water or stock
1 1/2 c. lentils
1 onion, chopped
2 t. curry powder
1 t. ginger
1 t. cumin

2 ribs celery, chopped (op-
    tional)
2 carrots, chopped (optional)
2-3 T oil (optional)
yogurt

Follow recipe for Split Pea Soup, except don't beat, and cook about 15-20 minutes. A combination soup may be made, using lentils, lima beans, and/or split peas.

## Mung Beans Soup*

4 c. boiling water or stock
1 1/2 c. mung beans
1 onion, diced

seasonings to taste
celery, carrots, diced (op-
    tional)

Slowly drop beans into boiling water. Lower heat and simmer until almost done (about 30 minutes). Add onion and any other vegetables and cook until beans are done. Add seasonings and let steep about 5 minutes.

## Soy Chili

3/4 c. soy grits
1 lg. onion, chopped
1 green pepper or jalapeno,
    chopped
2 cans tomato sauce or 6
    fresh tomatoes
3 c. cooked beans

3-4 T oil
1/2 lb. cheese, grated or
    shredded
1 T chili powder, or to taste
2 t. cumin
pinch of cayenne

Heat oil in large pan. Saute onion, pepper, and soy on low to medium heat, stirring to prevent soy from burning. After 5 minutes add tomato, beans, seasonings, and more water if mixture is too thick. Cover tightly and simmer about 15 minutes. Remove from heat. Add more chili powder if desired. Place cheese on top. Cover and let steep about 5 minutes.

## Potato Soup*

4 potatoes, finely diced
1 lg. onion (or scallions or
    leeks), finely chopped

2 c. milk
2 T tamari or 2 vegetable
    cubes

sea salt
pepper
dill

2 ribs celery, finely chopped
grated cheese, parsley, cress,
    or sprouts

Heat about 2 cups water while scrubbing potatoes. Don't peel, but cut out any bad spots. Dice very fine. Drop potatoes into hot water. Add enough water to just cover potatoes, if necessary. Cover tightly and cook until tender, about 20 minutes. Remove from heat, beat and mash to make smoother, although some lumps can remain. Add onion, celery, milk, and seasonings. Adjust consistency by the amount of milk you add. Reheat briefly if necessary. Cover and let steep about 5 minutes. Garnish with cheese or greens.

## Substitute Potato Soup*

4 c. stock
1 1/2 c. bulgur, barley, or
    buckwheat kasha
1 onion, chopped
1-2 c. milk, for desired con-
    sistency

sea salt
pepper
dill
2 ribs celery, finely chopped
    (optional)
grated cheese

Slowly pour bulgur into boiling stock. Once it resumes brisk boil, cover and simmer about 15 minutes. Add onion, or sauteed onion and celery, and seasonings. Cover and let steep 5 minutes. Garnish with cheese.

## Potato and Cheese Soup*

3 med. potatoes, unpeeled
    and diced finely
1/2 lb. cheddar or sharp
    cheese
1 1/2 c. milk, or to desired
    thickness
water to cover potatoes

1 onion, diced
1 green onion, or 4 chili pep-
    pers, diced
sea salt
pepper
oil

Saute potatoes in oil 5-10 minutes, until well glazed. Add onion and pepper and saute about 2-3 minutes more. Add water, cover, and cook until potatoes are almost tender. Add diced cheese, seasonings, and milk for desired consistency. Simmer until potatoes are done.

## Cheese Soup*

| | |
|---|---|
| 1/2 lb. cheese, diced (more if desired) | 2-3 T oil |
| 1 1/2 c. milk (or less for thicker soup) | 1-1 1/2 c. diced vegetables— onion, celery, green pepper, carrots, grated potato |
| 1/4 c. whole wheat or soy flour or mixture | 2 c. stock |
| | sea salt and pepper to taste |

Heat oil and saute vegetables about 5 minutes. Lower heat, sprinkle flour over mixture, stirring continuously about 3 minutes. Add more oil if necessary. Pour stock very slowly into mixture, continue to stir and simmer until thickened. Add milk, cheese, and seasonings. Stir well. Heat until cheese almost melted. This is a favorite and so easy to make!

## Egg Drop Soup

| | |
|---|---|
| 4 c. stock | 1 onion, finely chopped |
| 1 egg beaten | 1 T oil, if onion is sauteed |

When stock has come to a boil, add onion. Lower heat and cook about 5 more minutes covered. Pour beaten egg into stock, stir once and turn off heat.

## Vegetable Soup*

| | |
|---|---|
| 6 c. stock | 3 T oil, if some vegetables are sauteed |
| 2 onions | seasonings to taste: celery seed, dill, cumin, oregano, basil, bay leaf |
| 1 can tomatoes, or 4 fresh | |
| 4 c. fresh vegetables: swiss chard, celery, carrots, turnips, green beans, cabbage, spinach, frozen corn, or peas | 1 c. cooked noodles or soy grits (optional) |

In large pot saute vegetables such as onion, celery, and carrots. Set aside. In same pan, heat stock. Add sauteed vegetables, all other vegetables and noodles. Season and simmer covered until vegetables are cooked, but not soft, about 20 minutes. Season again, to taste, cover, and let steep about 5 minutes.

## Onion Soup*

6 med. onions, chopped
4 c. stock
sea salt

2-3 T oil
grated cheese and croutons

Saute onions until lightly brown. Add stock, stir, and simmer covered about 15 minutes. Season to taste. Garnish with cheese and croutons or crackers.

## Gazpacho

2 cans tomato, or about 6
   fresh
1 green pepper, finely diced
1 cucumber, finely diced
1 onion, finely diced
2 c. tomato juice

3 T wine vinegar
2 T oil
sea salt to taste
parsley, chives
1 clove garlic

This simplified version is good only if served cold. Make it only if you can get some ice cubes. Combine all ingredients and put about 6 ice cubes into mixture. Stir vigorously several minutes until quite cold. Remove remaining cubes. Serve at once.

## Cream Soup*

2 c. finely diced vegetables:
   celery, carrots, leeks, spinach, cress
1/2 c. milk (optional)
4 c. stock

3 T oil
1/2 c. flour
seasonings: sea salt, celery,
   cumin

Saute vegetables about 5 minutes, stirring frequently. Still at simmer, sprinkle flour over mixture. Keep stirring and add more oil if needed. Cook about 5 minutes. Slowly add stock, stirring constantly, until mixture starts to thicken. Add milk and seasonings and simmer 2 or 3 minutes. Let steep, covered, a few minutes. Garnish with cheese, sprouts, or whatever is available.

*Alternate method:* Saute vegetables in oil. Add stock and heat. Combine milk and flour until smooth and stir it into soup. Add seasonings.

## Minestrone

| | |
|---|---|
| 1 med. eggplant, diced | 3-4 T oil |
| 1 sm. cabbage, cut up (or chard) | 4 c. stock |
| | 3 tomatoes, cut up |
| 1 lg. onion, diced | seasonings: oregano, basil, bay |
| 1-2 c. beans, cooked, or 3/4 c. uncooked bulgur | leaf, sea salt |

In large pot saute eggplant and onion about 3 minutes. Add cabbage and saute about 3 more minutes, stirring occasionally. Stir in beans, add stock, and simmer 10-15 minutes. Add tomatoes and simmer 5 minutes. Season and remove from heat. Steep covered about 5 minutes. Garnish with grated cheese or sprouts. If you have a large cabbage, use half and use the rest as salad.

## Tuna Chowder

| | |
|---|---|
| 1 7-oz. can tuna | 3 potatoes, unpeeled and diced finely |
| 2 onions or chives, diced | |
| 3 T oil | water to cover |
| sea salt, celery seed, dill | chives, for garnish |

In large pot, saute potatoes and one onion about 5 minutes. Add water and bring to boil. Cover and simmer until potatoes almost tender, about 15 minutes. Add flaked tuna, the other onion, and seasonings. Stir in more water or milk if too thick, and cook until potatoes are tender. Garnish.

## Barszcz (Polish Beet Soup)

| | |
|---|---|
| 1 1/2-2 lbs. beets, sliced | 1/4 c. lemon juice |
| 2 carrots, diced | 1 T sugar |
| 1 potato, diced | 1 t. salt |
| 3 T instant celery flakes | 1/2 t. paprika |
| 1 T parsley flakes | 1 T oil |
| 1 onion, chopped fine | 4 hard boiled eggs, sliced |
| 1/4 t. garlic powder | 1 c. sour cream (optional) |
| 1/2 t. dill weed | |

Combine all vegetables and condiments with 6 cups water and bring to boil. Simmer covered 35 minutes, or until beets are tender. Stir occasionally. Add sliced eggs. Meat eaters may also add 1/2 pound thinly sliced kielbasa or pepperoni. Serve with rye or pumpernickel bread. Sour cream may be stirred in after cooking. Heat but do not boil cream.

# Main Courses

### Kasha and Beans with Cheese

| | |
|---|---|
| 1 1/2 c. kasha (buckwheat groats) | 2 T oil |
| 1 1/2 c. hot water | sea salt, cumin, tamari |
| 1 onion, diced | grated or sliced cheese |
| | 2 c. cooked beans |

Saute onion about 2-3 minutes. Add kasha and saute 3-4 minutes, stirring constantly, over low heat. Very slowly pour hot water into kasha, cover, and simmer about 12-15 minutes, until water is gone. Add beans and seasonings and simmer until beans are hot. Place cheese on top, turn off heat and cover, until cheese is melted.

### Kasha with Vegetables

| | |
|---|---|
| 2 c. kasha | 3 c. hot water, or 2 3/4 c. |
| 3-4 T oil | water and 1/4 c. tamari |
| 1 lg. onion, diced | 2 carrots, diced |
| 3 ribs celery, diced | 2 eggs, beaten |
| 1 green pepper, diced | sea salt, cumin, celery seed |

In large pan, saute vegetables about 4 minutes. Add kasha and saute 3-4 minutes more, stirring constantly. Add eggs, stirring. When eggs are done, in about 2 or 3 minutes, slowly add hot water, and seasonings. Cover and simmer 15 minutes, or until water is gone. Garnish with grated cheese, sprouts, or yogurt.

### Plain Kasha

| | |
|---|---|
| 2 c. kasha | 3-4 T oil |
| 3 c. hot water, or 2 3/4 c. | 2 eggs, beaten |
| water and 1/4 c. tamari | sea salt |

Over very low heat, pour kasha into an oiled pan. Add eggs and stir continuously about 2-3 minutes. Slowly add hot water and sea salt, stir, and simmer covered until water is absorbed, about 15 minutes. Uncover during last 5 minutes. Serve with sauteed vegetables, croquettes, as a rice substitute, or as a cereal at breakfast. Melt cheese on top before serving or stir in 1 tablespoon butter.

## Soy or Bean Tacos

12 tortillas or taco shells
1 lg. onion, diced
1 green pepper, diced
3/4 lb. cheese, grated
1/2 c. soy grits, or 2 c. cooked
    beans
6 oz. can tomato paste

water
2 c. bean sprouts, or chopped
    greens: lettuce, cress, etc.
oil
seasonings: 1 T chili powder,
    1 t. cumin, pinch cayenne

Saute onions and green pepper about 3 minutes. Add soy and saute 5 more minutes, stirring to prevent burning. Add more oil if needed. Stir in tomato paste, a like amount of water, and seasonings. Simmer covered about 10 minutes. Add more water if mixture seems dry. Remove from heat and let sit covered 5 minutes. When using beans, add to sauteed onions and pepper. Mash beans with fork while in skillet. Add seasonings and more water, if needed. Stir and simmer covered about 5 minutes. Serve over tacos. Sprinkle with cheese and sprouts. Otherwise, place tortilla in lightly oiled, heated skillet and warm 30 seconds on each side. Fold in half immediately and fill. Serve with cheese soup.

## Stuffed Green Peppers

4 lg. green peppers
water to fill pot 1/2"
1/2 c. plain kasha, or soy grits
1 onion, chopped

2 tomatoes, chopped
1 c. chopped cabbage, or swiss
    chard
seasonings

Bring water to boil. Place peppers on rack in pan, or use a pan-colander combination. Cover and steam 5 minutes. Make stuffing of rest of ingredients, sauteing onions 5 minutes and cabbage another 3, and mixing in tomatoes and seasonings. Saute another 6-8 minutes and fill peppers with the mixture. Steam 15-20 minutes. Garnish with cheese or yogurt. If you have no rack, place peppers in water and simmer covered.

## "Meat" Balls or Croquettes

1 1/2 c. "meat"—uncooked
    soy grits, bulgur or kasha

2 1/2 c. hot water
diced onion, nuts, or seeds

1 egg, beaten

1/4 c. flour

crumbs or wheat germ (optional)

sea salt, other seasonings

oil

Let water boil in deep pot (soy foams up as it cooks). Slowly pour in grain. When boiling resumes, simmer partly covered. When water disappears, 10-15 minutes, remove from heat, add 1/4 cup flour, and mix. Allow to cool a while. Add onions and nuts and stir. Mix in seasonings and egg. Crumbs may be mixed in a little at a time until a firm ball or patty can be formed. Fry in small amount of oil, not too hot. Pour a sauce over balls or croquettes, or melt cheese on top. Put in bread for a sandwich.

# Pasta

For 4 active people, allow 10 ounces of pasta, making about 6 cups cooked. Use your largest pot, fill it to within an inch of the top with water, add a teaspoon each of salt and oil, and let it come to a boil. Pour in noodles slowly or drop strands of spaghetti, letting them fall from your hand in a fan shape so that each piece is enveloped by water and boiling continues. Keep water boiling rapidly, uncovered. Stir with a fork almost continually to keep strands from sticking together. Time depends on the type of pasta; more for the thicker kinds and vice versa. Follow package directions, perhaps about 10 minutes for a medium type. At 8 minutes lift a few strands and taste. Too hard? Cook longer. You may like it at 9 minutes, or longer. Pour into a colander to drain—don't let it soak at all—and serve directly into each person's dish. Stir in sauce or other ingredients.

*Variations*

*Sauces:* See "Meat Sauce" and Tomato Sauce

*Cheese and milk:* Add 3/4 lb. diced cheese, 1/3 c. milk, and sea salt. Stir and cover until cheese melts.

*Tuna:* Add 1 c. tuna and mix well.

*Meat:* Non-vegetarians can add Meat Balls or Meat Sauce, under Ground Beef. (See p. 98)

**Macaroni and Cheese***

| | |
|---|---|
| 1/4 c. oil | 1 lg. tomato, chopped |
| 1/4 c. flour | 1 t. mustard |
| 1 t. salt | 1 lb. sharp cheese, cut up |
| 1/2 t. paprika | 6 c. cooked macaroni |
| 3 c. milk | |

Mix flour in heated oil. Slowly stir in milk and seasonings until mixture starts to boil. Lower heat, add tomatoes, and simmer a few minutes, stirring, until sauce thickens. Add mustard and cheese, continuing to stir until cheese softens. Add macaroni, mix together well, and heat thoroughly.

**Cheese and Pasta Mix**

| | |
|---|---|
| 1 onion, minced | 1/2 t. paprika |
| 2 T soy bacon bits | 1/2 t. marjoram |
| 1 T oil | 1/4 t. nutmeg |
| 6 c. cooked thin pasta, vermi-celli or linguini | 1 egg, beaten |
| | 1/2 c. cottage cheese |
| 1 c. sour cream | 4 slices American cheese, torn |
| 1 1/2 t. salt | in bits |

Saute onion and soy a few minutes. Set aside. Cook pasta according to package directions. Drain and return to the pot. Add onion and rest of ingredients, stirring well. Cover pot and place on very low heat until cheese is melted.

# Vegetables

Wash vegetables in a colander or rinse quickly under running water. Don't let them soak. Get rid of dirt but not nutrients. When in foreign countries that use human waste as fertilizers, treat unpeeled vegetables and fruit with the classic soaking (15 minutes) in potassium permanganate or bleach, 1 teaspoon to 1/2 gallon of water. Better yet, the modern wisdom is that ordinary weak detergent, without ammonia, is just as good. Wash the produce well, as if washing dishes, and rinse the solution completely with safe water. When using organic vegetables, you may find insects burrowed in the vegetables. Soak in salted water for a few minutes to coax them out. Artichokes, broccoli, and cauliflower should be particularly watched for this.

Cooking time for vegetables should be as short as is compatible with desired tenderness; this depends a lot on taste. The modern tendency is toward firmness. You add an extra dimension to your eating enjoyment when you chew into a textured piece of carrot or bean, rather than have it fall apart in your mouth. Exact times are difficult to predict. Factors are freshness, cooking conditions and preferences.

*Boiling:* Refer to the chart in the appendix. That list can be regarded as a guide; the only sure way is to take a taste at intervals. Use a very small quantity of salted water and let the steam in a closed pan do the cooking. You'll keep more of the nutrients and taste.

*Steaming:* Put a colander or rack in a pot (but not with a non-stick surface) and add water to 1/2" in depth. Put vegetables into the container, cover, and bring to boil. Steaming takes longer than boiling, perhaps 50 percent or more; slice vegetables thin to shorten time. If you carry neither colander or rack, you might be able to modify a container. Ian Hibell, the well-known bicycle tourist, perforated a smaller pan and hung it under the cover of his regular pot. He cooks meat in the lower part and the steam cooks vegetables in the upper part.

*Sauteeing:* Most boiled, steamed, or fresh vegetables may be sauteed a few minutes in butter, over medium low heat, to improve their flavor. Dice those and use about 1/4 cup oil for a panful. If you're cooking more than one, start with the hard ones—carrots, turnips—and add others that take less time or are chopped fine as you go along. Let taste be your guide.

*Garnishes:* Equal parts of yogurt and mayonnaise are good. So are tamari (use in sauteeing too), cream type sauces like cheese or white sauce, and the tomato-peanut butter sauce. Seasonings and spices may be sprinkled on or included in sauteeing.

### Sauteed Eggplant

| | |
|---|---|
| 1 eggplant, sliced 3/4" | 1/2 t. pepper |
| 1/4 c. flour | 1 t. turmeric |
| 1 t. salt | 1/4 c. oil |

Cook eggplant in covered pan for 7-9 minutes, or just before tender. Use just enough water to cover. Preheat oil over medium flame. Mix salt, pepper, and flour, and dredge cooked eggplant slices in mixture. Brown and let drain before serving.

### Eggplant Parmesan

1 lg. eggplant, unpeeled
1 lg. can tomatoes, or 5
  chopped
1 onion, diced
1 green pepper, diced
1 c. cornmeal or flour, or
  mixture
oil

3/4 lb. parmesan or cheddar
  cheese
seasonings: sea salt, garlic,
  oregano, basil, cumin,
  celery seed
pumpkin or sunflower seeds
  (optional)

Slice eggplant 1/2 inch. Dip in water, then into cornmeal, and saute both sides until just tender. Add small amounts of oil to prevent burning. Place aside on paper bag. In skillet, add more oil, and saute onion and green pepper about 5 minutes. Stir in tomatoes, seeds, and seasonings. Simmer covered about 6-10 minutes. Remove from heat. Layer eggplant into pan, spooning tomato over it, and the cheese over all. Cover and simmer to reheat and melt cheese.

### Zucchini Delight*

4 med. zucchini, diced
1 lg. onion, diced
2 cloves garlic
1 green pepper or 3 ribs
  celery, diced
4 tomatoes, chopped, or 1
  can tomatoes

seasonings: garlic, oregano,
  cumin, sea salt, celery seed
2 T tamari
sunflower seeds (optional)
cheese or yogurt garnish
oil

In preheated oiled skillet saute vegetables, except tomatoes, about 10 minutes. Stir occasionally. Add tomatoes, seeds, seasonings, and tamari, simmering 5-10 minutes longer. Melt slices of cheese on top or garnish with yogurt. For a complete meal, serve with kasha, noodles with oil and garlic, rice, or griddle cakes.

**Creamed Mushrooms***

| | |
|---|---|
| 1 lb. fresh mushrooms | 1 T parsley flakes |
| 3 T butter | 1/4 t. tarragon |
| 1 sm. onion, finely chopped | 1 c. sour cream or plain yo- |
| 2 T flour | gurt, or 1 c. bouillon |
| 1/2 t. salt | |

Rinse mushrooms well and slice lengthwise. Saute with onion over moderately low flame about 4 minutes. Sprinkle with flour and mix well. Add rest, mixing in cream slowly. Heat well and serve.

# Potatoes

Peel or not, as you wish. Most of the minerals are just under the skin. Cover completely with water after scrubbing well, add about 1 teaspoon salt and boil 20 to 35 minutes, depending on size. Cut large ones in half; sizes more or less equal cook evenly. At 15-20 minutes, test with a fork. If done, it will enter easily. Serve boiled potatoes with a cream sauce or simply add butter or sour cream.

*Mashed:* When well boiled, mash with fork. If unpeeled, cut them up before boiling to cope with the skin easier. Add about 1/2 cup milk and 1 teaspoon salt for 8 potatoes, while stirring. Melt in 1/4 stick or more of butter and stir in well.

*New Potatoes:* Use small ones and boil 15 minutes or until done. Melt butter, about 3-4 tablespoons, and warm 1 teaspoon lemon juice, 2 tablespoons instant parsley flakes, and 1/4 teaspoon nutmeg or mace, until the parsley is reconstituted. Pour over potatoes as garnish.

**Hash Browns**

| | |
|---|---|
| about 2 potatoes (3/4 lb.) per person | 1/4 c. oil |
| | 1/4 c. flour |
| sm. onion, chopped fine | 1 1/2 t. salt |
| 1/2 c. milk, coffee cream or buttermilk | 1/2 t. pepper |

Stop cooking potatoes when they are still firm but nearly done, about 15 minutes, depending on size. Cube about 1/4" or cut into small slices when cool enough to handle. Saute onion. Add milk and remainder of ingredients, mixing well but gently. Add potatoes. Turn over a few times without chopping at the mixture, to coat with flour and the rest. Don't pat. Fry over medium heat about 15 minutes, turning over occasionally. Cover pan between turnings if potatoes start drying out.

### Potato Salad with Hard Boiled Eggs

3 lbs. potatoes, with skins
1 t. salt
1/2 t. pepper
3 T soy bacon bits
1/4 c. vinegar
3 T sugar or honey
1/4 t. dry mustard

1 c. plain yogurt
1/4 c. oil
1 med. onion, or bunch scallions, chopped fine
1 sm. dill pickle, minced
6-8 hard boiled eggs, sliced

Cook potatoes. Slice fairly thin when they can be handled. In pot, warm oil and mix in rest of ingredients except eggs. Mix potatoes and eggs gently into the pan mixture.

### Potato Salad with Anise

3 lbs. potatoes, with skins
1 t. salt
1/2 t. pepper
1/4 t. anise seed, crushed
1/4 c. vinegar
1/4 c. dry wine

1/4 t. tarragon
1 T parsley flakes
1/8 t. garlic powder
1 bay leaf
1/4 c. oil

Cook potatoes. When they can be handled slice fairly thin. Warm oil in pot and mix in rest of the ingredients. Take off flame and let stand 5 or more minutes to blend in flavors and reconstitute parsley flakes. Pour dressing over slices or mix gently in pan until potatoes are well coated and the liquid absorbed.

### Potato Pancakes

4 lbs. potatoes, grated
1 onion, grated or minced
2 lg. eggs, well beaten
5 T flour

2 t. salt
1/4 t. pepper
1 T parsley
oil

Drain grated potatoes, pressing slightly. Mix with rest of ingredients, except oil. Drop batter into preheated oiled pan by large spoonfuls, flattening if necessary with back of spoon. Fry crisp on both sides over medium flame. Serve with tart applesauce, or raw or steamed vegetables. Garnish with plain yogurt or cheese.

# Rice

### Basic Recipe*

| | |
|---|---|
| 2 T oil | 1 t. salt |
| 1 sm. onion or 1/2 garlic | 1/4 t. pepper |
| clove, chopped fine | 1 t. parsley flakes |
| 2 c. long grained white rice | 1/4 t. thyme, cumin or savory, |
| 3 1/2 c. water | or pinch of saffron |
| 4 bouillon or vegetable cubes | |

Lightly brown onion and rice over medium flame. Add water and dissolve bouillon. Stir in condiments, cover, and bring to boil. Simmer 17 minutes. Most times given on packages are too long and the proportions too "wet." Take off heat and leave covered another few minutes. If for some reason the rice is uncooked at the end of that time, fluff it up a bit with a fork and put it back on very low heat until the water is absorbed. Don't take the lid off during cooking. Makes 5 1/2 cups. Bouillon or vegetable cubes may be chosen according to the kind of dish used with the rice. Meat eaters may use chicken cubes with fish dishes, or beef with meat dishes, for example. Spices would also depend on the rest of the meal. Skip them if your main dish is heavily spiced and needs a bland foil.

*Pilaf:* Add 1/4 cup each of toasted almonds and raisins, or 1/2 cup mushroom bits into the cooked rice, and fluff mixture with a fork. Try adding 1 teaspoon crushed orange peel also.

*Spanish:* Saute a green pepper and 3 ribs celery, chopped, in 2 tablespoons oil until just tender. Add 1 lb. canned tomatoes, 1 tablespoon chili powder, and a batch of cooked rice. Stir, bring to boil, and simmer over a very low flame 10 minutes.

### Fried Rice, India Style

| | |
|---|---|
| | 6 T oil |
| 2 c. brown rice, or converted | 1 sm. can garden peas, or |
| rice, or 1 1/2 c. rice and | fresh green beans |
| 1/2 c. soy grits | 1/2 c. nuts: cashews, almonds, |
| 3 3/4 c. water | sunflower seeds, or peanuts |

1/2 c. raisins
1 onion, diced
2 carrots, diced
2 ribs celery, diced
2 eggs, beaten

1/4 c. milk or water
2-3 T curry powder
1 t. ginger
1/3 c. tamari

Heat 3 tablespoons oil in pot. Add rice and saute, stirring, about 4 to 5 minutes. Add water, tamari, 1 teaspoon curry, and raisins, and bring to boil. Simmer covered about 35 minutes for brown and 15-20 minutes for converted rice. Heat 3 tablespoons oil in large pan; saute onion, carrots, and celery about 5 minutes. Add nuts, peas, rice mix, curry, and ginger. Cover and heat slowly about 5 minutes. Combine eggs with milk. Add to rice and stir until eggs are done, about 5 minutes. To make using only one pan: When rice is cooked, add onion, celery, carrots, nuts, peas, and seasonings, and simmer about 10 minutes. Add tamari or water if too dry. Stir occasionally. Add eggs and stir until done.

## Rice and Beans with Cheese

1 1/2 c. brown or converted
    rice
2 c. cooked beans
1 onion, diced
1 green pepper, diced (op-
    tional)

3 T oil
3 c. water
seasonings to taste: sea salt,
    cumin, celery seed, pinch
    cayenne
grated or sliced cheese

Saute onion and pepper 2-3 minutes. Add rice and saute 4 minutes, stirring constantly. Add water and bring to boil. Simmer covered until done, when water is gone. Don't stir rice while cooking. When cooked, stir in beans and seasonings. Simmer covered until beans are hot. Place cheese on top, turn off heat and cover until cheese is melted.

## Salads

### Taboulli*

1 c. cracked wheat (bulgur)
1 sm. bunch parsley, chopped
1/2 c. green onions, leeks or
    chives, chopped

4 tomatoes, chopped
1 t. sea salt
1/4 c. olive oil, or other
1/3 c. lemon juice
pinch of dill

Soak wheat in water 20-30 minutes. Drain well and put in bowl. Mix in most of parsley, all the onions, tomatoes, sea salt, and dill. Add lemon juice and oil. Toss well to mix thoroughly, then add mint. Before serving, garnish with remaining parsley or mint. Watercress or nasturtium leaves may substitute for parsley, and wild onions, garlic, or wild mint might be available for foraging.

### Spinach Salad*

2 lbs. fresh spinach
feta cheese or Roquefort
sunflower seeds
cucumber

tomatoes, chopped
sprouts
chives
oil and vinegar, or yogurt

Wash and drain spinach, break into small pieces, and toss with rest of ingredients.

### Carrot Salad

4 carrots, grated or finely
   diced
1/2 c. raisins
sea salt to taste

1/2 c. mayonnaise, or 1/2 c.
   yogurt and 1 T lemon
   juice or vinegar, or oil and
   vinegar

Combine all ingredients.

Photo by the author

**Spinach-Avocado Salad**

3/4 lb. spinach
sm. head bibb lettuce, or
    equivalent lettuce

4 hard boiled eggs, chopped
1 avocado, diced 1/2"
1/2-1 c. yogurt

Tear up greens and combine well with rest of ingredients.

**Tomato Salad**

4 tomatoes, in small chunks
1 green pepper, diced
4 scallions, or sm. onion,
    sliced thin
few drops Tabasco

1 T vinegar
2 t. fresh ginger, shaved, or
    1/2 t. ground ginger
1 t. salt

Combine all ingredients well.

**Fresh Fruit Salad***

Allow about 1/2 pound fruit per person. Combine any assortment, but try to complement tastes: a citrus, a fleshy sweet,
berries in season (or pick them), banana, tart apple. Cut into bite
sized pieces and stir in a cup of plain yogurt. Sprinkle lightly with
cinnamon, mace, or nutmeg, and mix well. Serve with small
wedges of sharp cheese.

**Jacque's Salad*** (from Jacque and Ken Proctor who traveled
around the world by bicycle)

cucumber
green pepper
hard boiled egg
canned tuna
tomatoes

celery
lettuce
ripe olives
salad dressing of olive oil
    and lemon, mixed

Tear, chop, and combine. Make a meal of it with a Knorr instant
soup and chunks of French bread. Buy vegetables only fresh from
farmers' stands.

# Dressings and Sauces

Each recipe given is for four servings or approximately 1−1 1/2
cups.

## Yogurt-Mayonnaise

1/2 c. yogurt
3/4 c. mayonnaise
1/2 t. vinegar

to taste: chili powder, garlic,
   sea salt, celery seed, dill,
   cumin, basil

Combine well.

## Homemade Mayonnaise

1 sm. egg, beaten
1/2 t. honey
1/4 t. sea salt

1/2 c. oil
1 T lemon juice or vinegar

Rapidly beat egg, honey, salt, and half of lemon juice. Use a whisk and mix very thoroughly. Very slowly begin adding oil, whisking continually. Stop adding oil occasionally, beating thoroughly before continuing. Finish with the remaining lemon. You may also add in finely diced green onion, diced olives, horseradish, or chives.

## Vinegar-Oil

1/4 c. vinegar
1/2 t. garlic powder
1/4 t. pepper

1 t. ground mustard
1/2 t. salt
1/2 c. oil

Dissolve mustard and garlic completely into vinegar. Mix together with rest of ingredients thoroughly.

## Yogurt-Tamari

Combine 1 cup yogurt, 1 tablespoon tamari, and seasonings to taste.

## Roquefort Dressing

1/4 c. roquefort cheese
1 t. lemon juice
1 t. sugar or honey
1/2 t. salt

1/8 t. garlic powder
1/2 t. dry minced onion, reconstituted in 1 T water
1 c. plain yogurt

Mash cheese and combine with rest of ingredients.

## White Sauce

3 T margarine or butter          1/2 t. salt
1/4 c. flour                     dash pepper
1 1/4 c. milk

Melt margarine, stir in flour, and cook on low heat 2-3 minutes. Add milk slowly as mixture warms to a near boil, while stirring. Add salt and pepper and any flavorings, such as grated cheese, parsley, a couple drops of Tabasco, or 1/8 teaspoon nutmeg, curry, or garlic powder.

## Tomato Sauce

onion, diced                     1 can tomatoes, or 4 fresh,
garlic, diced                        chopped
green pepper (optional)          6 oz. can tomato paste
oil                              oregano, cumin, chili powder
sea salt                         water

Saute onion and garlic about 5 minutes. Mix in rest, using water for desired consistency. Simmer covered 10-15 minutes.

## Tamari and Beer

1 c. tamari
1/2 c. beer
1/2 t. ginger

Combine ingredients; thin with water if too strong. Good with soy, bulgur, kasha balls, or patties.

## "Meat Sauce"

Same as tomato sauce, except saute 1 cup soy grits with vegetables.

## Cheese Sauce

4 T oil                          1/2-3/4 lb. cheese, diced
4 T flour                        sea salt
2 c. fresh milk

In heated oil, slowly add flour, stirring. When well blended, add milk slowly, continuing to stir. Simmer until it begins to thicken, about 10 minutes. Add cheese and remove from heat. Stir and leave covered until cheese melts. Season to taste.

## Thousand Island Dressing

1 T instant minced onion
1/8 t. garlic powder
1 T lemon juice
1 sm. pickle, chopped fine

2 T ketchup
4 drops Tabasco
1 t. sugar

Combine onion, garlic, and lemon juice. Stir in rest of ingredients. Let stand 10 minutes to reconstitute dry ingredients.

## Garlic-Mustard Sauce

1/8 t. garlic powder
1 t. ground mustard
1 T water

1 c. plain yogurt
1 t. salt

Mix garlic, mustard, and water. Stir into yogurt and salt. Let stand 10 minutes to reconstitute dry ingredients. Serve with vegetable dishes and potatoes.

The following are mainly meat sauces:

## Gravy

1 T flour
1/2 t. salt

1 c. milk or bouillon
1/4 t. pepper

Combine flour and seasonings with liquid, and add slowly to leftover fat from browning beef in pan. Stir to make smooth with whisk.
*Mushroom:* Stir in mushroom bits, drained, and 1 tablespoon Worcestershire sauce.
*Cheese:* Stir in 1/2 cup grated cheese, until melted.
*Spices:* Stir in to suit, 1/4 to 1/2 teaspoon.

## Steak Sauce

2 T butter
2 scallions, sliced thin, or
    2 T onion soup mix
1 clove garlic, minced

1/4 c. dry wine
1/2 t. Worcestershire sauce
1 T dehydrated parsley
1/2 t. salt

Simmer scallions and garlic a few minutes in butter. Stir in remaining ingredients, bring to boil, and cook over low flame until wine is somewhat evaporated and liquid reduced.

**Bordelaise Sauce**

handful of fresh mushrooms,
   chopped
1 T butter
3 T flour dissolved in 1/2 c.
   cold water
2 t. lemon juice

2 T dry wine
1 beef bouillon cube, dissolved in 1/2 c. hot water
1/2 t. tarragon
1/2 t. salt
1/4 t. pepper

Saute mushrooms over low heat a few minutes. Stir in bouillon and flour. Bring to boil. Stir in rest and simmer until somewhat thickened. Serve over kabobs or beef.

**Tartar Sauce**

1 c. plain yogurt
1 T parsley flakes
1 t. tarragon
1/2 t. ground mustard
1/8 t. garlic powder

1/2 t. onion flakes
1 t. vinegar
1 t. oil
1 t. lemon juice
sm. sour pickle, minced

Combine all ingredients well. Let stand 10 minutes to reconstitute dry ingredients.

**Seafood Sauce**

1 T vinegar
1 t. ground mustard
1 t. salt
1/4 t. pepper
1/8 t. garlic powder
1/4 c. parsley

3/4 c. oil
1 t. lemon juice
few drops Tabasco
1 onion, minced
1/4 t. tarragon

Whisk together first four ingredients. Add oil gradually, still whisking. Stir in the rest. Serve over seafood or as a dip.

**Tomato-Peanut Butter Sauce**

6 oz. can tomato paste
2 c. chicken bouillon
1 t. salt

1/4 t. pepper
1/2 c. peanut butter
1 T instant minced onion

Heat tomato in bouillon. Stir in rest into the simmering sauce. Use to cook chicken, or over zucchini and similar vegetables.

**Sweet-Sour Jam Sauce**

1 c. jam of any fruit on tart
    side—apricot, sour cherry,
    crabapple, citrus
1/2 c. water

2 T ketchup
2 T vinegar
1 t. cornstarch dissolved in
    2 t. water

Combine first four ingredients. Bring to boil, stirring. Add corn-starch and simmer until thickened. Serve over ham.

Photo by the author

# Desserts

There is no problem finding desserts in the United States. The problem is often the opposite, resisting the ubiquitous Carvels and the candy counters in stores. My favorite nemesis is a bakery, its sweet smells and even more seductive sights drawing me like a fly to spilled honey.

The selection of desserts is limited here to a few fruit desserts and puddings. Almost any store has packaged puddings that need only milk for preparation. Don't be put off by their directions to chill; they're just as good lukewarm and semi-set.

For me beverages are very simple. I drink water, tea, or coffee, and occasionally buy a milkshake during the day. The evening hours are often a license for a beer or two. None of these need a recipe.

## Cherry Sauce

1/3 c. sugar
3 T cornstarch
1 c. orange juice
3/4 c. dry wine or 1/4 c.
  cherry liqueur

8 oz. can sweet cherries, with
  juice

Combine sugar and cornstarch. Add orange juice slowly, stirring vigorously, then add wine. Heat over medium heat until thickened, still stirring. When boiling, stir in undrained cherries.

### Preserves-Nut Sauce

handful of almonds, or other
   nut meats, chopped
2 T butter or margarine

1 c. any fruit preserves
1/4 t. cinnamon
1 oz. lemon juice

Brown nuts lightly in butter. Add preserves, cinnamon, and lemon, and heat, stirring, until liquified. Pour over various desserts, as well as over ham or pork.

### Preserves-Wine Sauce

8 oz. any fruit preserves
1/4 c. sweet wine
1/4 t. vanilla extract

Simmer preserves and wine, stirring, until completely liquified. Stir in extract. Pour over various desserts or ham.

### Creamy Rice Pudding

1 pt. milk
1/8 t. salt
3/8 c. rice
1/4 c. raisins

1/2 c. evaporated milk
1 egg, slightly beaten
1/2 t. vanilla
1/4 c. sugar

Heat milk and salt over medium flame until warm. Stir in rice. Before the boiling point, lower heat, and simmer 15 minutes. Stir occasionally. Add raisins and cook until rice is done, another 5 minutes or so. Add one ounce of the evaporated milk and cook a few minutes longer. In a separate bowl combine egg, sugar, vanilla, and rest of evaporated milk. Stir some of the rice mixture into the egg mixture. Add the contents of the bowl into the pan, stir, and cook slowly until the pudding thickens.

### Simple Rice Dessert

Make extra cooked rice when making dinner. Don't add spice or onion to it. For each cup of rice, mix one cup of cut fruit, fresh or unsweetened canned, a half cup of sugar, and one beaten egg. Fashion into flat cakes and fry in butter until light golden. Top with a sweet sauce, whipped cream, or a flaming fruit. You may add raisins or sprinkle with nuts.

## Chocolate Pudding

2 T cornstarch
1/2 c. sugar
4 T cocoa, all purpose
2 c. milk

Mix dry ingredients. Add milk, while stirring. Bring to boil over medium heat. Simmer 3 minutes. Allow to cool before serving.

## Chocolate Mousse

1/2 lb. semi-sweet chocolate
2 eggs, separated
pinch salt
1 c. heavy cream

Make this simple yet elegant dessert some evening to impress your fellow campers, but practice first at home a few times to get the knack; it's tricky. Dice the chocolate with a knife or pound into pieces. Chocolate bits may be used, and are usually cheaper than solid chocolate. Place in a bowl, which is set into a pan of hot water. Whip the whites and salt until stiff. Whip the cream until stiff. Set both aside. When chocolate melts, stir in 2 teaspoons water. You should have a thick fudge-like mixture. Mix in a bit more water if it's too thick to stir. Let chocolate cool somewhat, but not get set. Beat yolks and add the chocolate slowly, mixing until smooth. Mix the chocolate-egg combination into whites gently but thoroughly. Fold half of the whipped cream into the chocolate mixture, but do not mix. It should have a marbled appearance. If a refrigerator is available to be used for a half hour, let the mousse set in it. If not, a closed container in a stream might do it. But without cooling, the mousse will still be delicious. Top with remaining whipped cream in individual servings. A half jigger of liqueur or fruit brandy may be mixed in, at the chocolate-yolk mixture stage, for a scrumptious touch.

## Pears in Wine

1 lb. can pears (save juice)
1/4 c. sweet wine—marsala,
    port or liqueur

Boil juice until it's reduced to a half or a third. Add wine, stir, and simmer another few minutes. Pour over pears.

## Fruit in Butter

Allow 1/4 to 1/2 pound of canned fruit per person, preferably unsweetened, cut into bite-sized pieces. Drain juice and warm in about 1/2 stick of melted butter, into which are mixed 1/2 teaspoon cinnamon, 1/8 teaspoon nutmeg or mace, or 1/2 teaspoon ground anise seed. An additional pinch of ginger with pears or apples is also tasty. Add fruit and warm well.

*Fresh fruit:* Mix with 1/4 to 1/2 cup water, depending on their pulpiness, the spices, and 1/4 teaspoon grated lemon rind. Simmer until fruit is tender. Keep the fruit on the firm side; it should take only a few minutes. Stir in melted butter.

Top individual portions of fruit with whipped cream, ice cream, or a box of prepared custard. Make this dessert first and let it stand while you make your meal. Its taste will improve.

## Banana Fritters

| | |
|---|---|
| 3 T flour | 1/8 t. baking powder |
| 2 T cornstarch | 1 T butter, softened |
| 1 T sugar | 8 bananas, sliced lengthwise, |
| 1/2 c. milk | then in half |
| 1 egg, beaten | 2 T oil |

Combine first 4 ingredients. Stir in the next 3, in order. Dip banana slices and brown in preheated oil for a few minutes. Top with whipped cream or a sweet sauce.

## Flaming Bananas*

| | |
|---|---|
| 3 T butter | 1 t. cinnamon |
| 3 T sugar | 1/4 t. nutmeg |
| 4 bananas, sliced | 2 oz. dark rum |

Melt butter over medium flame and add sugar. Cook about 1 minute. Add banana slices and cook, turning, until softened. Add spices and rum and mix in well; remove from stove. Set aflame either in pan or on individual plates. Spoon the sauce over bananas when flame subsides. May be served over ice cream or sponge cake.

## Flaming Fruit

Almost any canned fruit can be prepared this way. Drain fruit and set aside. Cook juice at a fast simmer until reduced to half its volume. Cut fruit bite-sized. Warm in juice. Top with about 1 ounce of warmed brandy or liqueur per serving and set aflame.

## Basic Sweet Sauce*

| | |
|---|---|
| 3/4 c. sugar | 2 T butter |
| 1 c. water | dash of salt |
| 1 T cornstarch | |

Combine all ingredients and bring to boil while stirring. Variations of flavors can be created by adding 1 teaspoon cinnamon, nutmeg, or vanilla, or by crumbling in a plain chocolate candy bar (cut down on sugar). Brandy, wine, or instant coffee are other possibilities. A handful of raisins added to the boiling mixture makes raisin sauce.

## Caramel Sauce*

Combine 1 cup sugar with 1/2 cup water and cook over medium heat, stirring. When sugar is dissolved don't stir any longer. Heat at low boil until the solution turns light brown. Stir in another 1/2 cup water and heat until of medium density. Especially good for making old fashioned candied apples on a stick.

## Rice Cakes

| | |
|---|---|
| 2 c. cooked, plain rice (add salt only) | 2 t. baking powder |
| 3 eggs, separated | 1/2 c. sugar |
| 6 oz. water | 1 t. cinnamon |
| 1/2 c. flour | 1/2 t. nutmeg |
| | oil |

Let rice cool. Beat egg yolks well. Add water and beat a few minutes longer. Combine flour and baking powder with a tossing motion, and mix into the yolks, making a thick batter. Whip egg whites until stiff. Fold into batter. In a separate bowl, toss together rice with sugar and spices. Don't let this stand around, as the sugar soon becomes syrup and will drain out. Stir and fold the rice mixture into the batter gently but thoroughly. You'll have a settling of the rice-sugar, but this is normal; don't try to mix it. Spoon about a 2-3 inch puddle of the rice batter into a preheated, sizzling pan. Just wipe a non-stick pan with an oiled paper. In a regular pan, use a minimum of oil, a tablespoon or so. Keep cakes separate in pan. Fry to a golden brown, about 2 minutes on each side. Stir the batter each time before spooning. Place cakes on folds of toilet paper or napkins to absorb oil. Sprinkle with sugar and let cool and air dry. Store away and use as road snacks.

(Following recipes from June Clifton)

### Candied Apples*

4 apples, unpeeled
4 t. honey
1 t. cinnamon

Wash and core apples, but don't break through the apple's bottom, so juices won't seep out. Place apples, top side up, in 1/2" boiling water, cover, and steam about 5 minutes. Put honey and cinnamon in each apple and steam 5 more minutes.

### Cold Fruit Soup

1 cantaloupe or melon
1 sm. can frozen orange juice
2 bananas, sliced, or strawberries, or 2 apples,
   chopped

pinch of cinnamon
touch of lime or lemon
mint

Cut melon in half, scoop out small chunks, and put in container. Include juice. Combine with rest of ingredients and garnish with mint. Use empty shells as serving dishes.

### Banana Treat*

4 bananas
4 t. wheat germ
2 t. honey
4 t. unsweetened coconut, or
   chopped nuts

In skillet with 1/2" boiling water, place unpeeled bananas. Lower heat, cover, and steam about 2 minutes. Peel bananas and place onto a strip of tin foil, large enough to wrap around. Cut a canal about 1/2" wide down the length of each banana, to hold the other ingredients. Fill each with honey first, then others. Wrap up and replace in skillet, steaming 2-3 minutes. If you have a broiler available, place under it, unfoiled.

## Ambrosia*

8 oranges, peeled and cut up
6 bananas, sliced
1 c. unsweetened coconut
2 T honey (optional)

Combine all ingredients.

## Snacks*

Maintain your energy with natural sweets, preferably.
*Fruits:* Buy unsulphured and naturally dried: apples, apricots, raisins, prunes, peaches, figs. Mix in a grab bag.
*Hulled nuts and seeds:* These can't be stored too long if kept in warm or damp conditions. They'll become rancid because of their high fat content. Mix with raisins or fruit to make "gorp."
*Peanut butter balls:* Combine 1 cup peanut butter, 1 cup honey, 1 3/4 to 2 cups powdered milk, 1 cup nuts or seeds. Make into 1" balls. Eat before the heat affects them.
*Fresh fruit:* Any firm type that can stand bouncing on two wheel travel. Avoid ripe peaches, for example; they bruise easily and may turn to pulp.

## Beverages

Try herb or mint teas. Pour boiling water over a large pinch and let steep 5 minutes. Black strap molasses and hot water is good for breakfast.

## Fudge

6 oz. evaporated milk          pinch salt
3 T butter                     1 t. vanilla
2 c. sugar                     handful of chopped nuts or
1/2 lb. chocolate chips            raisins

Combine milk, butter, and sugar. Bring to a boil quickly, stirring. Simmer a few minutes until sugar is well dissolved. Take off the fire, let it cool a bit, and stir in rest of ingredients. Stir slowly until it begins to set. Pour into lightly oiled pan (wipe with oiled paper). Cut it up before it's fully hard. Use as energy snacks.

# One-Person Recipes

Chicken breasts, boned or otherwise, lend themselves well to one-person dishes. You can buy a single breast from a butcher shop, and can usually talk a supermarket butcher into packaging just one for you. A wide variety of dishes can then be made from the breast. A quarter to a half pound of ground meat can also be bought from the same sources. So can a ham slice.

Other foods convenient for one that can be found in most groceries—some raw, others in cans—include soups, cheeses, ham bits, broiled lobster tail, certain delicatessen meats, and salad items.

The recipes listed in this chapter are especially suitable for solo cooking. But many others in the rest of the book can be adapted to single person use. Those are identified by an asterisk. In those, just divide all ingredients by four or substitute the equivalent amount of dehydrated ingredients. Others in the book might also be adapted if you're willing to skip a hard-to-buy ingredient, or if you can find a substitute.

## Oriental Steak

3/8 lb. steak, sliced very thin
1 sm. green pepper, cut 1/2"
  by 2"
2 t. oil
1 T flour
1/2 c. water

1 T soy sauce
1/2 t. sugar
1/4 t. salt
dash ground ginger
1 med tomato, cut in chunks

Brown meat and pepper over medium flame. Set meat aside. Saute pepper over low flame until just tender. Replace meat and add rest. Saute 5 minutes. Serve over rice.

### Chili Con Carne

1/4 lb. ground beef
1 sm. onion, chopped
8 oz. canned beans, kidney or
   pinto

8 oz. can tomato sauce
1/2 t. chili powder
pinch garlic powder
pinch cumin

Brown beef and drain. Stir in rest; simmer slowly 3/4 hour. Stir occasionally. Serve over rice.

### Meatballs in Tomato Sauce

1/4 lb. ground beef
1 sm. egg, beaten
1 t. instant minced onion
dash pepper

1/4 t. salt
8 oz. can tomato sauce
dash each of basil and oregano

Form small meatballs of first 5 ingredients. Brown over medium flame and drain fat. Add rest, stir, and simmer 15 minutes. Serve over spaghetti or rice, or add dumplings in last 10 minutes.

### Ground Beef and Corn

1/4 lb. ground beef
1 sm. onion, sliced
1 lg. potato, diced
1/2 c. beef bouillon

1/2 t. salt
pinch pepper
pinch thyme
8 oz. can creamed corn

Brown beef and onion and drain. Add rest, except corn. Stir and bring to boil. Put potatoes under water. Simmer 15 minutes or until potato is just done. Mix in corn and simmer 5 minutes.

### Creamed Chicken

1 sm. chicken breast
3/4 c. chicken bouillon
1 t. cornstarch
1/2 c. milk or plain yogurt
1 T instant minced onion
1 T celery flakes

1/2 t. salt
1 whole clove
pinch garlic
1 t. paprika
1 sm. can mixed vegetables,
   drained

Bring chicken to boil in bouillon. Cover and cook at fast simmer 20 minutes, or until almost tender. Dissolve cornstarch in milk and stir into pot. Add condiments. Add vegetables, cover, and simmer 10 minutes over low heat. Dumplings may be added last 10 minutes, or serve over noodles or rice. Remove clove. A few fresh or dried mushrooms may be added at the end also. If canned chicken is used, skip the first 20 minutes cooking.

**Chicken Omelet**

| | |
|---|---|
| 1 sm. onion, chopped fine | 1 slice bread, crumbled |
| 1/2 t. parsley flakes | 2-3 egg omelet |
| pinch garlic powder | 1 can prepared chicken |
| 2 T oil | a la king |

Saute onion, parsley, and garlic in oil. Add bread and mix in well to soak up oil. Make omelet and fold in the bread mixture. Heat chicken and pour over omelet.

Photo by the author

### Chicken Spaghetti

8 oz. can tomato sauce
1 sm. onion, diced
pinch garlic powder
1/4 t. salt
pinch pepper, basil, and
  oregano

1 sm. can cooked chicken,
  drained
1/2 t. cornstarch

Combine tomato and condiments and simmer 10-15 minutes. Add chicken and heat through. Dissolve cornstarch in a little water and stir into mixture, until thickened. Serve over spaghetti.

### Chicken Cacciatore

1/2 chicken breast
2 t. oil
pinch garlic powder
1 sm. onion, quartered, and
  leaves separated
1 8 oz. can tomato sauce

1/4 t. salt
pinch pepper
1/4 t. oregano
pinch basil or thyme
a few fresh or dried mushrooms, chopped

Brown chicken with garlic and onion. Add rest of ingredients, except mushrooms. Bring to boil and simmer covered until chicken is done, about 30 minutes. Add mushrooms and simmer, uncovered, 5-10 minutes. Serve over spaghetti or rice.

### Chicken Hash

1 sm. onion, chopped
2 t. oil
1 sm. can cooked chicken or
  turkey, broken up
1 sm. can cooked sweet potato,
  sliced

1 sm. can mushrooms, drained
1/2 t. salt
pinch pepper
1/2 c. milk

Saute onion in oil. Stir in rest, milk last. Heat and serve over rice.

### Chicken with Soup Sauce

1 c. water
1 t. cornstarch
2 t. soy sauce
1 T chicken soup mix

1 sm. can cooked chicken or
  turkey
3 drops Tabasco

Mix water with soup mix, bring to boil, and simmer 10 minutes. Mix 1 T water with cornstarch and soy. Add to cooked soup. Simmer until mixture is thickened. Add meat and Tabasco and heat well. Serve over rice or bread, or rolled in a crepe.

## Chicken and Plums

| | |
|---|---|
| 1/2 chicken breast | 1 1/2 t. lemon juice |
| 1 sm. onion, sliced | 2 t. water |
| 1/2 clove garlic, minced | 2 ripe plums, sliced |
| 1 1/2 t. soy sauce | 1 t. sugar |

Brown chicken, skin side down. Drain any fat and turn chicken over. Add rest all at once and cover. Simmer about 30 minutes or until chicken is tender. Cook 10 minutes longer with cover off.

## Creamed Chicken Livers

| | |
|---|---|
| 1/4 lb. chicken livers, sliced 1/2" | 1/4 t. Worcestershire sauce |
| | 1/4 t. salt |
| 1 small onion, sliced thin | pinch pepper |
| 1 T oil | 1/2 c. plain yogurt |

Brown liver and onions over medium low heat. Lower flame, add seasonings, and cook 10 minutes covered. Stir in yogurt and heat well but short of a boil. Serve over noodles or rice. Artificial bacon bits or chopped boiled eggs can be mixed in with liver.

## Peppers Stuffed with Chicken and Mushrooms (from Dennis Devlin)

| | |
|---|---|
| 1 c. cooked rice, using chicken bouillon, 1 t. oil, bay leaf | 1 sm. can cooked chicken |
| 1/2 t. instant onion flakes | 1 sm. can or jar mushrooms |
| 1/4 t. salt | 1 or 2 green peppers |

When rice is cooked, stir in chicken and rest, except peppers. Cook covered 10 minutes. Cut peppers in half, along the stem axis, and remove stem and seeds. Place halves on top of the covered pot, with open sides down to warm peppers. When cooked, serve in pepper halves.

*Curried Chicken:* Delete bay leaf and onion in above. Mix in 1 teaspoon curry powder to bouillon before cooking rice. A few dashes of Tabasco can also be added.

*Variations without green pepper:* Use bay leaf, curry, and salt to make rice. Combine with small can oysters, 1/4 teaspoon garlic powder, 1/2 teaspoon pepper, and mushrooms. Cook as above. About 6 fresh oysters or clams may be used instead, cooking 15 minutes after adding to rice. Other meats—canned turkey (or fresh from deli counter), tuna or beef, 1/4-1/2 pound, browned—may be substituted. A small can of vegetables, drained, may also be added.

## Pork Chop and Sauerkraut

| | |
|---|---|
| 1 pork chop, 5/8-3/4" thick | 1 T water |
| 1 sm. can (1/2 lb.) sauerkraut | 1 sm. onion, chopped |
| 1/2 t. caraway seed | 8 oz. jar applesauce |
| 1/4 t. salt | 2 t. sugar |
| dash pepper | |

Brown chop on medium flame. Drain any fat. Remove chop. Drain sauerkraut, place in skillet, and mix in caraway and water. Place chop on top. Sprinkle chop with salt and pepper and cover with mixed applesauce, onion, and sugar. Simmer covered 1/2 hour or until pork is done. Add more water if necessary (if steam escapes).

## Pork Chop with Apple and Pineapple

| | |
|---|---|
| 1 pork chop, 1/2-3/4 lb. | 1/4 t. ginger |
| 1 apple, sliced in eighths | 1 t. sugar |
| 1/2 t. soy sauce | 1/2 c. chunk pineapple, with |
| 1 t. vinegar | juice |

Trim chops and render fat. Brown chop and discard fat. Place apple slices on chop, skin side down. Pour on soy, vinegar, and a tablespoon of water. Sprinkle sugar on apple and add ginger into liquid in pan. Cover and simmer over low flame 20 minutes. Add pineapple over chop and cook uncovered 20 minutes longer. Baste chop with sauce occasionally.

### Curried Pork, Corn and Rice

| | |
|---|---|
| 1/2 lb pork, cubed 1/2" | 1/2 t. salt |
| 1 sm. onion, chopped fine | pinch pepper |
| 1/4 c. rice | 1/2 t. curry powder |
| 1 t. oil | 1 tomato, chopped |
| 1/2 c. water | 1 sm. can niblet corn, drained |

Brown pork, onion, and rice. Stir in water and condiments. Bring to boil and place vegetables on top of chop, without stirring. Cover and simmer 25 minutes, or until rice is done.

### Spiced Ham Slice

| | |
|---|---|
| 3/8 lb. thick ham slice | 1 t. oil |
| 4 oz. orange juice | pinch ground cloves |
| 1 T sugar | 1/4 t. ground ginger |
| 1/2 t. vinegar | 1/4 t. dry mustard |

Combine all ingredients in plastic bag and let marinate 1 hour or longer. Place in pan and simmer 25 minutes, turning over midway. Serve with rice.

### Ham, Pineapple, and Green Beans (from Dennis Devlin)

| | |
|---|---|
| 1 c. cooked rice, as in Peppers Stuffed with Chicken recipe | 1 sm. can beans or mixed vegetables |
| 1 sm. can ham | 1 sm. can pineapple |

Combine rice, ham, and beans, and simmer until warm, about 10 minutes. Top with pineapple last few minutes. Piece of boiled ham from deli counter or Spam may be used.

### Ham and Pineapple

| | |
|---|---|
| 1/4 lb. cooked ham | 2 T ketchup |
| 1 t. oil | 1/4 t. ground mustard |
| 8 oz. pineapple tidbits, un-sweetened, with juice | pinch nutmeg |
| | 1 t. cornstarch |
| sm. green pepper, cut in strips | 1 T cold water |

Saute ham in oil. Drain pineapple juice on meat. Add pepper, ketchup, mustard, and nutmeg. Stir and simmer covered 8 minutes. Mix cornstarch in water and add with pineapple to mixture. Stir and heat until thickened. Serve over rice.

### Toasted Cheese and Ham

4 slices rye bread
2 pats oleo
1/4 lb. ham slice, cubed
1 hard boiled egg, diced
2 slices American cheese, or sm. piece cheddar, diced

1 t. oil (optional)
1 T ketchup
few drops Tabasco
1/4 t. salt
1/4 t. minced onion flakes

Spread oleo on one side of bread. Place 2 slices, oleo side down, over medium flame in frying pan. You may just let oil be heated and coat the pan if you have no oleo. Combine rest of ingredients in a separate container and place over the bread, topping with torn strips of cheese. Cover with the other slices of bread, oleo side up. Let the bottom get toasted well, turn over, and toast other side. Cover pan partly to help retain heat.

### Ham and Squash

1 sm. onion, chopped
2 t. oil
1/4 t. salt
pinch garlic powder
pkg. frozen squash slices, thawed

1/4 c. beer
1/4 lb. ham slice, cubed
sm. tomato, in rough chunks

Saute onion. Add squash and stir-fry a few minutes. Add rest and simmer 10 minutes, stirring occasionally. Serve over rice. Sliced carrots, okra, or other vegetables may also be used.

### Ham and Spiced Beans

1 can beans in tomato sauce
lg. ripe peach, cut in chunks
1 t. vinegar
2 t. sugar
1 t. Worcestershire sauce

1/2 t. ground mustard
pinch ground clove
1/4 t. cinnamon
1 t. instant minced onion
1/4 lb. cooked ham

Combine all but ham. Stir and heat well. Mix in ham, cover, and simmer about 10 minutes.

**Shrimp and Egg**

sm. can shrimp, bite sized

1 hard boiled egg, chopped

1 t. oil

1 T ketchup

sm. pinch onion powder

pinch salt

1 serving cooked rice

Mix all but rice thoroughly. When rice is just cooked, stir in shrimp mixture. Heat a bit longer to warm up shrimp.

# APPENDIX

## Some Hints

The cooking wisdom of the ages—the real discoveries and short cuts, as well as the pet beliefs, old wives tales, and prejudices—have been passed on from the first barbeques in caves. Here are a number that people swear by, some with solid scientific basis, others based on folklore:

Buy margarine, instead of butter, if you anticipate having any left over. It'll keep.

Cheddar or Monterey Jack cheese keeps well and is useful for cooking as well as lunches.

Heat canned goods right in the can. Open the lid to let out steam, but leave the top on while heating. Opening it first will save you burnt fingers later.

Save vegetable cooking water for sauces, but drain water from canned goods. Canned water contains a disproportionate amount of additives and often has an unpleasant taste.

You can maintain the whiteness of potatoes by adding a tablespoon of vinegar to the pot of cooking water, as well as the usual salt.

Make extra rice at supper, without onion or spice, for a rice pudding dessert later.

Add a small pinch of nutmeg or cinnamon to tea or coffee for flavor.

Don't pat diced potatoes when cooking; you'll make them mashed.

"Never substitute green olives when black are called for in a recipe," advises Dennis Devlin.

For better browning, make hash browns or French fries from regular potatoes, not new.

To remove discoloration in aluminum pots, boil apple peelings in them.

When the inside of a pan gets dark and stained, remove by boiling water and vinegar, about a tablespoon per quart of water.

An old trick is to add a little vinegar, about 1/2 teaspoon per quart, to the water in which a tough cut of meat is being stewed.

Eggs for French toast can be mixed with water instead of milk.

Some people add a few drops of lemon juice to water when cooking rice, claiming that the rice will be whiter and the grains will separate better.

You can keep boiling eggs from cracking by first poking a hole in the large end with a pin.

Dry mustard balls up when it bounces around on the road. Pack it compactly within crumpled toilet paper or with rice. But you'll have to pick out those grains of rice when using it.

Buy leafy spices to keep freshness and to prevent balling up.

Put a few pinches of rice into the salt container to prevent clumping from moisture.

Horseradish and ketchup, mixed in a ratio of one to five, equals chili sauce.

Keep recipes or cookbook in waterproof or plastic envelope, and keep them away from the wet area when cooking.

Add salt to water when boiling eggs to aid in peeling them.

Keep food warm by either placing the dish in a paper bag and then into a sleeping bag, or by putting it into another, larger pot of hot water. Also, if you have a flat top for the pan that is on the stove, you can place your finished dish on it to keep warm.

Save the spongy plastic container in which most supermarkets package meats. They're good to use as throwaway cutting boards for such vegetables as celery and onion.

About 1/4 cup of wine can be added to almost any meat recipe, substituting for another liquid.

In stews, add herbs and spices in the last half hour of cooking.

Juice from apples or other fruit offers a taste variation in recipes calling for wine.

Consider vermouth when cooking in wine. Its herbs add an interesting flavor, which is delicate for fish and chicken especially.

Don't stir any more than you have to while cooking, at least not vigorously. The extra oxygen you incorporate into the food will break down some food elements and affect nutrients.

To avoid lumping, always dissolve flour in a bit of cold water before adding it to a hot mixture.

Don't overheat any kind of oil or fat, to the point of smoking. It will break down.

Honey can be used in place of sugar in the same amounts. Blend it into one of the liquid ingredients of the recipe to make the mixing easier.

A pinch of salt in egg whites helps stiffen them when beating. Also, they stiffen better when warm than cold. The opposite is true for heavy cream.

Be careful of canned goods overseas. If air rushes out with a pop when you open a can, don't use it.

Don't buy fresh milk in backward countries. Pasteurization may be suspect or nonexistent. Bring along powdered milk for recipes.

# Staples for Cooking on the Road

These are the staple foods I use on the road. Many of them need not be bought except when required for the evening meal. Keep the unused balance in sturdy plastic bags. Take other staples out of their original containers and store them in plastic also, to save space and weight.

Cream of wheat and oatmeal are the most compact cereals to carry, in terms of initial weight versus the volume that they produce.

Cornstarch or arrowroot can substitute for flour, when used for thickening. Gauge the amount of flour you'd ordinarily use—for pancakes or fried breads—and carry about three days worth in a plastic bottle. Try to replenish it, as well as sugar and salt, through individuals and cafes rather than by buying a large package.

cereal

long-grained rice

pasta

dried mushrooms (optional)

powdered milk (optional)

raisins

honey (optional)

sugar

flour

corn meal (optional)

cornstarch

baking powder

baking soda

vegetable oil

lemon juice (the kind in a plastic lemon)

vinegar

cooking wine (optional)

bread

jam

peanut butter

instant coffee (optional)

tea bags

emergency ration (dried soup)

drink mix (only overseas, to mask the taste of treated water)

# Foods for Hot Weather Riding

In the old days, before nutrition became the special province of universities and government agencies, our grandparents ate immense, heavy meals before going to work. They ate steaks or bacon with piles of onioned hash browns, stacks of pancakes covered with eggs, French toast on the side, cold buttermilk and hot coffee to wash it down, and perhaps a large bowl of oatmeal or farina to bind it all together. Then they'd start their day's hard labor: plowing, chopping trees, lifting heavy loads, washing a week's dirty clothes by hand.

Today we're more scientific. A bicycle racer—or tourist on a long ride—is apt to balance his diet carefully for desireable nutrients, vitamins, and minerals, load his body with a controlled amount of carbohydrates and drink specially prepared liquids. Does it help cyclists in their day's labor better than did our grandparents' diet for theirs? Perhaps. At least, they weren't as anxious or guilty about what they ate.

Without getting too concerned about control, I do believe some of the common sense rules are in order: eating small amounts at frequent intervals, rather than having a large meal, for example. It's best to avoid fats and proteins like hard cooked eggs and hamburgers during the day's ride. Eat those at the evening meal. Stay away from carbonated drinks and milk products. Concentrate on energy-providing sugars and carbohydrates (see rice cake recipe, for example).

I eat a lot of fruit for their sugars, minerals, and natural fiber, and because they taste good. Bananas are bikers' favorites because they replenish the body's potassium. But other fruits are also rich in that mineral: papayas, avocados, dried figs and apricots, dates, raisins, oranges, grapefruit, pineapple and prune juices, cantalope, strawberries, and cooked rhubarb. All of those are full of simple sugars and other nutrients.

"Gorp" is the bicyclists' name for a snack mixture that can be nibbled out of your hand. Any combination of ingredients is legitimate, depending on taste. No formal recipe is needed. My gorp depends on what's available and relatively cheap. In Turkey, for example, it was nuts. There, shelled pistachios and other exotics cost less than fifty cents a pound. I mixed those precious nuts with raisins and other dried fruit, which were also abundant. Cyclists in America like to add M&M candy, peanuts, and various seeds such as pumpkin or sunflower.

Some people may be bothered by the diuretic effect of fruit (promoting urine flow; but not the same as a diarrheic), but it's a small price to pay for the benefits. Certain kinds of nuts—those with a high fat content or tending to bitterness—may not agree with individuals. These adjustments will have to be made, of course.

A weak electrolyte solution—about a third strength—is useful for anticipated periods of exertion. Any commercial type will do. Mix with fruit juices to make it more palatable. The solutions usually contain some dextrose and salt. If you have hypertension or kidney problems, check with your doctor. The extra salts may be harmful.

Most Americans eat enough salt not to have to worry about its loss, but in very hard riding you might add a pinch to a bottle of plain water or diluted juice. Water is the most important ingredient under conditions of hot weather and exertion. Drink lots of it, in small amounts, before you feel thirsty.

As in swimming or any other strenuous sports, don't exercise immediately after eating any kind of meal. If you must be off in a hurry, eat only easily digested foods, in small amounts at intervals, rather than all at once. And pace yourself and rest frequently. Diet alone won't do it.

# High Altitude Cooking

High altitude cooking is not a subject I know well, since I've not done a great amount of it. That might be because of the character of bicycle touring. A pass or mountain range is what bicyclists usually negotiate as a goal during a day's ride, coasting down to a campround in the lower area by evening. The high places usually lack stores and most of us balk at shopping and loading our bikes *before* climbing.

However, it's possible to spend a few days in the mountains and a road camper should be familiar with the effect of altitude on cooking. It's well known that such cooking takes longer than at sea level. Atmospheric pressure gets lower as you go higher, and water will boil sooner. But the food is being cooked at a lower temperature.

How much longer the cooking should be, exactly, seems difficult to discover. Neither individuals with experience at high altitudes nor the Cooperative Extension Service of Colorado State University could provide me with specific guides. That university has published a number of pamphlets, most of which deal with baking. By extrapolation of some of this data, and from suggestions of backpackers, I've devised the following table and a list of general hints:

## Relative Cooking Times for Various Altitudes

| Feet: | sea level | 1-2,000 | 2-3,000 | 3-4,000 | 4-5,000* |
|---|---|---|---|---|---|
| Relative time: | 10 min. | 12.5 min. | 15 min. | 17.5 min. | 20 min. |

*Above 5,000 feet, you'll need either a pressure cooker or the patience of Job.

## High Altitude Hints

● To sidestep the problem, substitute fast cooking techniques for normal ones. Use instant rice and pre-cooked meals that need only warming. Cut potatoes and vegetables into small bite-sized cubes instead of cooking them whole.

● Avoid most fresh meats, especially those that need long cooking times. Depend more on eggs and cheese, and eat a greater proportion of breads and dry snacks.

● The fuel tank in your stove will probably need less pressure. The ten strokes you used at sea level may be worth fifteen. Best to start the stove with a lower pressure and work up as needed.

● A double boiler becomes so inefficient at altitudes greater than 4,000 feet that you may as well cook in a regular pot.

● There's a tendency for flour to become drier at higher altitudes. If you stay at high altitudes long enough for that to happen, mix more liquid into your batter for fried bread, dumplings, and pancakes. At about 4,000 feet add ten percent more liquid. At 8,000 feet add twenty-five percent. However, if you make no change the results will not be calamitous, unless you're at a very high elevation: your breads will just rise more than usual.

● In addition to increasing the liquids, decrease the amount of baking powder by the same percentage. Since the atmospheric pressure decreases, your leavening action increases proportionately. That is, for each teaspoon in the recipe, decrease the powder by about 1/8 teaspoon at 4,000 and by 1/4 teaspoon at 8,000.

● Lower the flame somewhat when frying. If you don't, the outside of the food will be browned too much while the inside will be undercooked. You'll have to cook longer overall, of course. Let a taste test be your guide.

# Spices and Condiments

Spices stimulate the senses with their taste and smell. They also arouse the imagination with their hints of exploration and the exotic. America itself was discovered in a search for the spice lands, and wars were fought to open caravan routes to the East. Spices seem to go with travel.

A few judicious sprinklings of the right spices will enliven almost any meal. Discretion is the key; if a little enhances, more doesn't make it better.

Here are spices and condiments I consider basic to my road cooking. The amounts indicated would do, approximately, for four-person recipes. When amounts are not indicated, they are widely variable and would depend on the kind of recipe in which they are being used.

| | | | |
|---|---|---|---|
| basil | 1/4 to 1/2 t. | rosemary | 1/4 to 1/2 t. |
| oregano | 1/8 to 1/2 t. | sage | 1/4 t. |
| bay leaf | 1 leaf | caraway seed | 1/2 to 1 t. |
| ground cumin | 1/8 to 1/2 t. | curry powder | 1 to 3 T |
| thyme | 1/8 to 1/4 t. | cinnamon | |
| ground clove | 1/4 t. | nutmeg | 1/4 to 1/2 t. |
| whole clove | 4 to 6 | ginger | 1/4 to 1/2 t. |
| marjoram | 1/2 t. | tarragon | 1/4 t. |
| salt | 1 t. | ketchup | (optional) |
| pepper | 1/4 t. | chili sauce | (optional) |
| peppercorns | 3 to 4 | soy sauce | |
| paprika | 1/4 to 1 t. | Worcestershire sauce | 1 t. |
| dry onion flakes | | Tabasco | |
| parsley flakes | | onion soup mix | 2 T |
| whole garlic | 1 clove | chicken bouillon cubes | |
| garlic powder | 1/8 t. | beef bouillon cubes | |
| dry mustard | 1/4 to 1 t. | vanilla | (optional) |

The onion soup mix can be used in place of onion. Bring vanilla if you plan to make rice pudding.

You may occasionally see a recipe calling for bouquet garni. This is a mixture of leaves of parsley (two parts), marjoram (one), thyme (two), and bay leaf (one-half) tied in a bag and left in a stew. After cooking, it's removed. You can use ground versions of the spices and put them directly into the pot, the amount totaling about a teaspoonful.

A commercial poultry seasoning is made up of thyme, sage, marjoram, rosemary, and nutmeg. Use a pinch of each in a recipe calling for it.

There's no need for packing whole packages of spices, except those used often or in a large volume each time, such as curry powder or parsley flakes. Instead, fill 35mm film cans about half full of the spices and three to five ounce plastic bottles with the condiments.

Double up on some spices in packing—a dozen whole cloves with ground cloves, a dozen peppercorns with bay leaf—to save space.

Paste labels on the cans and cover the labels with scotch tape; paint or grease pencil soon wears off.

Crush all dry leaf spices between the fingers, just before use, except bay leaf.

## Addresses of Selected Cooking Equipment Suppliers

Eastern Mountain Sports
Vose Farm Road
Peterborough, NH 03458

Eze-Lap Diamond Products
P.O. Box 229
Westminster, CA 92683

Great World Wilderness Outfitters
250 Farms Village Road
West Simsbury, CT 06092

Moor and Mountain
63 Park Street
Andover, MA 01810

Mountain Safety Research
631 South 96th Street
Seattle, WA 98108

Recreational Equipment, Inc.
P.O. Box C-88125
Seattle, WA 98188
(a cooperative)

## Abbreviations

| | | | |
|---|---|---|---|
| t. | teaspoon | min. | minute |
| T | tablespoon | hr. | hour |
| oz. | ounce | sm. | small |
| lb. | pound | med. | medium |
| c. | cup | lg. | large |
| pt. | pint | pkg. | package |
| qt. | quart | | |

## Common Measures

1 T = 3 t.
2 T = 1 oz. liquid or fat
1 c. = 16 T
1 c. = 8 oz.

Although not very commonly used nowadays, can sizes are occasionally referred to in recipes.

| can no. | weight (oz.) | cups |
|---------|--------------|------|
| 1 | 11 | 1-1/3 |
| 1-1/2 | 16 | 2 |
| 2 | 20 | 2-1/2 |
| 2-1/2 | 28 | 3-1/2 |
| 3 | 33 | 4 |
| 10 | 106 | 13 |

## Weights and Measures of Various Foods

| | volume | weight |
|---|--------|--------|
| med. onion, chopped | 1/2 c. | 5 oz. |
| sm. green pepper, chopped | 1/2 c. | 4-1/2 oz. |
| 3 lg. scallions, sliced | 1/2 c. | 3-1/2 oz. |
| 3 lg. ribs celery, chopped | 1 c. | 4-1/2 oz. |
| 8 oz. can tomato sauce | 1 c. | |
| med. apple, chopped | 1 c. | 4 oz. |
| 15 oz. pkg. raisins | 3 c. | |
| med. lemon | 2-1/2 T juice | |
| med. orange | 1/2 c. juice | |
| 1 lb. butter or oleo | 2 c. | |
| stick (1/4 lb.) butter | 8 T | |
| 1 lb. solid cheese | 4 c. grated | |
| 1 lb. cottage cheese | 2 c. | |
| 1 lg. chicken breast (1-1/4 lb.) | 2 c. bite sized | 10 oz. boned |
| typical chicken, whole | | 2-1/2 to 3-1/2 lbs. |
| 1 lb. rice | 2-1/3 c. dry | |
| 1 c. rice (7 oz. weight) | 3-3/4 c. cooked | |
| 1 lb. macaroni, many pastas | 3-4 c. dry | |

Some weights and measures are approximate

## Substitutions and Equivalents

| | |
|---|---|
| 1 c. fresh milk | 4 T powdered + 1 c. water |
| 1 c. fresh milk | 1/2 c. evaporated milk + 1/2 c. water |
| 1 c. sour milk, buttermilk or plain yogurt | 1c. milk + 1 T lemon juice or vinegar (let stand 5 mins.) |
| can cream-type soup (for cooking) | 2 T flour mixed in 6 oz. cold water, heated and mixed with 2 bouillon cubes |
| 1 T cornstarch | 2 T flour |
| 1 T arrowroot | 3 T flour |
| 1 c. sugar | 1 c. honey, and reduce recipe liquid by 1/4 cup |
| 1 c. sugar | 1 c. brown sugar, firmly packed |
| 1 T orange peel | 1 T juice, or grated peel of 1 med. orange |
| 1 t. lemon peel | 1 t. juice, or grated peel of 1 med. lemon |
| lemon juice (for cooking) | vinegar, in same amount |
| 1 c. canned tomatoes | 1-1/3 fresh tomatoes, chopped; increase simmering 5-10 mins. |
| 1 c. tomato juice | 1/2 c. tomato sauce + 1/2 c. water |
| 1 c. ketchup or chili sauce | 1 c. tomato sauce + 2 T vinegar, and 1/2 c. sugar (for ketchup), or few drops tabasco (chili sauce) |
| 1 t. dehydrated parsley | 1 t. fresh parsley, chopped |
| 1/4 c. dehydrated celery flakes | 1/2 c. fresh (2 ribs), chopped |
| 1 T instant minced onion | 1 sm. onion, chopped (2 T) |
| 1 t. onion powder | 1 med. onion, chopped (4 T) |
| 1/8 t. garlic powder | 1 med. clove garlic, minced |
| 1 t. dry mustard | 1 T prepared mustard |
| 1/4 t. ground ginger | 1 t. fresh ginger, chopped or shaved |
| 1 T mint | 1/4 c. fresh mint, chopped |
| most dried herbs | 3-4 times as much of fresh herbs |

# Glossary

A number of these definitions are discussed in detail in other chapters, as indicated.

*al dente*        Firm to the bite, as opposed to soft cooked. Usually referred to when cooking pasta.

*baste*        To spoon juices from the pan onto the meat or other ingredients. Often used in pan braising and frying, to prevent drying, and to spread flavor of juices.

*batter*        A mixture of flour, other solids, and liquids.

*beat*        See page 44.

*blend*        To mix, fairly gently.

*bouillon*        A clear soup of chicken, beef, or vegetable flavor. Also dry concentrates in cube form, which when dissolved in hot water make an equivalent of a clear bouillon soup.

*braise*        To simmer meat in a pan, covered, with some liquid, replacing any liquid lost from evaporation.

*bread*        To coat with bread crumbs, as fish or chicken, preparatory to frying.

*chop*        See page 43.

*coat*        Cover meat or other ingredients, usually with

flour or egg, preparatory to frying. It's convenient to place dry ingredients and meat in a plastic bag and shake the contents.

*combine*    To mix.

*condiments*    Any seasonings, as salt, spices, soy sauce, or mint, that add aroma or taste.

*dice*    See page 43.

*dissolve*    To melt, as a bouillon cube in hot water.

*double boiler*    Two pots, one fitted inside the other. The outer one holds water that is heated, and the inner one the food. Cooking is consequently gentler, by means of transferred heat.

*dredge*    To coat.

*fold*    See page 44.

*fry*    To cook in oil or fat.

*grate*    To cut an ingredient into very small particles, as in grated cheese. Usually not possible without the use of a grater. Grating releases more flavor than shredding.

*julienne*    To cut into thin strips, usually such solid vegetables as carrots. Size is variable, about 1/4" by two or three.

*marinade*    See page 62 and 109.

*mince*    See page 43.

*pan broil*    Like braising, but with little or no oil and uncovered. Fat is drained as it collects. On non-stick surfaces, no oil at all is used. Only tender meats are suitable for this process. Tougher meats should be braised, stewed, or tenderized.

*parboil*    To boil food for a short time (a minute or two) in preheated water.

*pinch*    The amount you can pick up between two fingers, about 1/8 teaspoon.

*poach*    To cook eggs, sometimes other ingredients, in hot liquid.

| | |
|---|---|
| *render* | To melt fat by heating over low flame. |
| *saute* | See page 46. |
| *score* | Cut slightly, as in cutting the edges of meat chops to keep them from curling while frying. |
| *sear* | See page 46. |
| *shred* | To cut an ingredient with a knife or shredder, into small pieces. Pieces are larger and coarser than in grating. |
| *sift* | See page 44. |
| *simmer* | See page 45. |
| *steam* | To cook with the steam of boiling water, usually in a double boiler. |
| *stew* | To cook over a low flame in a liquid base at a low simmer for an extended time. |
| *stock* | Liquid that is released by, or is left from, cooking meats or vegetables. |
| *stiffen* | See page 44. |
| *tenderize* | See page 62. |
| *toss* | Mix by lifting lightly, taking care not to crush ingredients. |
| *whip* | Beat rapidly. See page 44. |

# Index

**A**

Abbreviations, list of, in recipes, 189
Additives, 58, 78 *See also* Natural foods; Nutrition
Addresses of suppliers, 189
Alcohol. *See* Fuel
Avocado-spinach salad, 156

**B**

Baking:
  oven, 10, 125
  powder, 125
  of quick-breads, 44
Beans:
  and Canadian bacon, 108
  chili con carne, 92
  and franks, 99-100
  with ground beef and cheese, 93
  and kasha with cheese, 145
  and Polish sausage, 107
  and pork chops, 103
  and rice with cheese, 154
  spiced, and ham, 176
  in stuffed green peppers, 146
  tacos, 146
Beating, 44
Beef:
  in beer, 82-83
  chipped, with cheese, 87

  corned, and cabbage, 85
  corned, hash, 86
  corned, and onions, 85
  creamed chipped, 87
  curry, 90-91
  Irish stew, 84
  liver and onions, 88
  oriental, 169
  pepper steak, 82
  pot roast, 82
  spiced, with vegetables, 80-81
  steak, 80
  steak in mushroom sauce, 81
  steak in pita bread, 81
  stew, 83
  stir-fry, with vegetables, 80
  stroganoff, 84-85
  *See also* Ground beef
Beet soup (barszcz), 144
Beverages, 162, 168
Breads:
  Chapati, 132
  dumplings, 132
  as extenders, 125
  French toast, 128
  fried, 125
  fritters, 131
  hoe cakes, 131
  hush puppies, 131
  *See also* Pancakes

Blazo, 25
Browning, 46
Brussels sprouts and ham and
    cheese, 105
Bulgar:
    "meat" balls, 146
    potato soup, 141
    substitute potato soup, 141
    taboulle, 154
Butane. *See* Fuel

## C

Cabbage:
    corned beef and, 85
    and franks, 100
    minestrone soup, 144
    and picnic ham, 104
    stuffed, 98
Campfires, disadvantages of, 24-25,
    34
Campsite, selection of, 37-38
Can sizes, 190
Carrot salad, 155
Check list, equipment, 4-5
Cheese:
    blintzes, 130
    with chipped beef, 87
    eggplant parmesan, 150
    macaroni and, 148
    parmesan, 150
    and pasta mix, 148
    sauce, 92
    soup and potato, 141
    toasted, and ham, 176
Chicken:
    and bananas, 116
    basic cooking, 110
    Brunswick stew, 115
    buying of, 110
    cacciatore, 116, 172
    Chinese, 114
    chop suey, 114
    creamed, 170
    in cream sauce, 113
    crisp-skin, 111
    curry, 49, 111, 174
    eggs Foo Yung, 115

fried, 111
hash, 172
livers, 173
Lo Mein, 86
omelet, 171
in one-person dishes, 169
and plums, 173
with rice, 112-13
with soup sauce, 172
sour cream, 113
spaghetti, 172
spiced, 112
and spices, 111
stir-fry, 111
in stuffed peppers, 173
sweet curry, 111
sweet-sour, 114
tomato-peanut butter, 111
in wine, 111
Chopping, techniques of, 43
Colander, collapsible, 11
Coleman:
    Backpacker stove, 28-29, 30, 31-
    32, 34-35
    fuel, 25, 30
Condiments. *See* Spices
Cook and assistant, 36-37
Cooking:
    in cold weather, 29
    definitions of terms, 191-193
    practice, 48
    in rain, 40
    sequence of operations, 39, 51,
    59
    timing, 45
    in wind, 29-30
    *See also,* Stoves
Corn and creamed ham, 104
Costs. *See* Economy
Crepes, 126, 129

## D

Desserts, 162
    chocolate mousse, 164
    chocolate pudding, 164
    creamy rice pudding, 163
    fudge, 168

rice cakes, 166
simple rice, 163
snacks, 168
*See also,* Fruit
Dicing, 43
Dishwashing, 52-54
Double boiler, 34

**E**

Economy:
  buying in volume, 66
  in campground selection, 66
  cost accounting, 67-68
  through extenders, 63-64
  of group travel, 68
  overseas, 67
  in shopping, 62, 64-66
  through substitution, 64-65
Eggplant:
  and meatballs, 97
  minestrone soup, 144
  parmesan, 150
  with pork and lamb, 108
  sauteed, 149
Egg(s):
  basic cooking, 127
  boiled, 135
  -chicken Foo Yung, 115
  creamed, 136
  -drop soup, 142
  fried, 135
  Mexican ranch, 135
  omelets, 127, 132-34
  poached, 134
  potato salad, with, 152
  scrambled, 134
  and shrimp, 177
Emergency rations, 19
Equipment, 3
  check list, 4-5
  non-essentials, 10-11
  packing of, 14-16
  selection of, 5
Equivalents, of ingredients, 189
Extenders:
  breads, 125
  with meat, 78-79

**F**

Fish:
  buying of, 117
  chowder, 118
  fried, 118
  sardine sandwiches, 122
  salmon patties, 120
  tuna a la king, 120
  tuna casserole, 119
  tuna chowder, 144
  tuna or salmon croquettes, 120
Folding in, 44
Food:
  carrying of, 23
  freeze-dried, use of, 20
  hot weather, 182-84
  junk, 61
  overnight storage of, 55
  pre-packaging of, 19
  sources of, 19
  spoilage, 56
  staples, list of, 181-82
  substitution of ingredients, 50,
    77, 189
  *See also,* Shopping
Frankfurter(s):
  and beans, 99-100
  and cabbage, 100
  and rice chili, 101
  and sauerkraut in beer, 100
  spaghetti, 100
Fruit:
  ambrosia, 168
  avocado-spinach salad, 156
  banana fritters, 165
  banana treat, 167
  in butter, 165
  candied apples, 167
  chicken and banana, 116
  chicken and plums, 173
  flaming, 165
  with ground beef, 96
  ham and pineapple, 175
  pears in wine, 164
  salad, 156
  soup, 167

Fudge, 168
Fuel:
    additives in, 25
    alcohol, 26, 32
    bottle, 14-15, 28
    gas cartridges (butane, LP, pro-
    pane), 26-27, 32, 35
    kerosene, 25-26
    other fuels, 31
    unleaded gas, 30-31, 32
    white gas (Coleman, Blazo), 25,
    27, 32, 34
    See also, Stoves

**G**

Garbage disposal, 54, 55
Garnishes. See Sauces
Gas cartridges. See Fuel
Gaz-Bluet stove, 27
Grains, 124, 127, 137. See also,
    Rice, Kasha, Soy, Bulgar
Green pepper. See Pepper
Ground beef:
    beans and cheese, 93
    and celery, 94
    chili, 92, 170
    Chinese meatballs, 97
    chop suey, 96
    and corn, 170
    and eggplant, 97
    with fruit, 96
    golabki (stuffed cabbage), 98
    hamburgers, 78
    Jambalaya, 119
    macaroni and cheese, 94
    meatballs for spaghetti, 98
    meatballs in tomato sauce, 170
    meat sauce for spaghetti, 98
    Mexican, 93
    Mexican cumin, 50
    and noodle, 95
    sloppy Joe, 93
    spiced, 95
    Stroganoff, 95
    Swedish meatballs, 97
    and vegetables, 94
    See also, Beef

Ground pork:
    balls, 106
    meat sauce for spaghetti, 98
    Mexican cumin, 50
    spiced, 95
    See also, Pork
Group cooking, 36

**H**

Ham:
    bigos, 108
    Brussels sprouts and cheese, 105
    creamed, and corn, 104
    creamed, with mushrooms, 104
    Lo Mein, 86
    and noodles, 104
    and pasta mix, 105
    picnic, and cabbage, 104
    and pineapple, 175
    with rice, 106
    spiced, 175
    and spiced beans, 176
    and squash, 176
    and toasted cheese, 176
    See also, Pork

Hamburger. See Ground beef
High altitude cooking, 184-85
Hints, cooking, 179-181

**K**

Kasha:
    and beans with cheese, 145
    "meat" balls, 146
    plain, 145
    stuffed green peppers, 146
    substitute potato soup, 141
    with vegetables, 145
Kerosene. See Fuel
Kitchen, organization of, 39
Knife:
    kind to buy, 11
    sharpening stone, 11

**L**                                      .

Lamb:
    curry, 89
    kabob, 89
    kidneys, 89

and pork, with eggplant, 108
-soy meatballs, 90
LP gas. *See* Fuel

**M**

Macaroni:
  and cheese, 148
  ground beef and cheese, 94
  *See also* Pasta
Marinades, 62, 161
Mayonnaise, homemade, 157
Measures, 43-44, 190
Meat:
  braising, 79
  extenders, 22, 78
  lessening dependence on, 78
  pan broiling, 79
  preparation time, 79
  *See also specific meats:* Beef;
  Pork; etc.
Meatless meals. *See* Natural foods
Menu planning. *See* Shopping
Mess kit, 7, 9, 10
Mincing, techniques of, 43
MSR/GK stove, 28, 31, 35
Mushrooms:
  creamed, 150
  and creamed ham, 104

**N**

Natural foods, 69
  carbohydrate content of, 71
  foraging for, 72
  meal preparation, 71
  meat substitutes, 70
  pre-packing of, 70
  shopping for, 69-70
  soup making, 73
  sprouts, 64, 72-73
  storing of, 70-71
Non-stick surfaces, 6, 8-9, 10, 53
Noodles. *See* Pasta
Nutrition, 61, 137.

**O**

One-person cooking, 59, 169. *See*
also recipes in book marked with
an asterisk
One-pot meals:
  and costs, 63
  defined, 51
  with pasta, 50
Onion(s), 138
  and corned beef, 85
  liver and, 88
  soup, 143
Optimus stoves:
  Mousetrap, 35
  8R, 28, 30
  99, 31
  111B, 28
Organic food. *See* Natural foods
Organ meats, 63

**P**

Packing equipment, 14-16
Pancakes:
  basic cooking, 125-26
  blintzes, 130
  buckwheat, 128, 129
  buttermilk, 129
  corn meal, 129
  crepes, 126, 129
  crepes suzettes, 130
  griddle cakes, 128
  nalesniki (Polish), 130
  potato, 152
  sweet milk, 129
  wheatcakes, 129
Panniers, 15
Pasta:
  basic cooking, 147
  as filler, 137
  variations, 147
Pepper (green):
  steak, 82
  stuffed with chicken, 173
  stuffed with grain, 146
Phoebus stoves 625 and 725; 28,
  30-33, 34
Plastic products, 12-13, 15-16
Polish sausage (kielbasa). *See*
  Sausage

Pork:
  with apple and pineapple, 174
  apple sauce, 101
  basic cooking, 101
  Canadian bacon and beans, 108
  chops and beans, 103
  chops, Chinese, 102
  chops with rice, 103
  chops with sour sauce, 103
  curried, 175
  with fried rice, 109
  with fruit, 101
  and lamb, with eggplant, 108
  and sauerkraut, 174
  stew, 102
  stir-fried, 101
  sweet-sour, 102
  tomato and onions, 101
  *See also* Ham; Ground pork
Potato, 138-139
  basic cooking, 151
  corned beef hash, 86
  hash browns, 151
  mashed, 151
  new, 151
  pancakes, 152
  salad with anise, 152
  salad with eggs, 152
  soup, 140
Pots and pans, 6-8, 9-10, 14, 16,
  45-46
Primus Grasshopper stove, 27
Propane. *See* Fuel

**Q**

Quick-breads. *See* Breads

**R**

Rain, cooking in, 40
Rice:
  basic recipe, 153
  and beans with cheese, 154
  cakes, 166
  fried, 109
  fried, India style, 153
  pilaf, 153
  types of, 137
  Spanish, 153

**S**

Safety practices, 30, 39, 40
Salads, 154-56
Sanitation, 52, 54-55
Sauce(s) and dressing(s):
  Bordelaise, 160
  cheese, 92, 158
  crepes, 130
  garlic-mustard, 159
  garnishes for vegetables, 149
  gravy, 159
  "meat," 158
  roquefort, 157
  sea food, 160
  steak, 159
  sweet-sour jam, 161
  tamari and beer, 158
  tartar, 160
  Thousand Island, 159
  tomato, 158
  tomato-peanut butter, 111, 160
  vinegar-oil, 157
  white sauce, 158
  yogurt-mayonnaise, 157
  yogurt-tamari, 157
Sauces, sweet:
  basic, 166
  caramel, 166
  cherry, 162
  preserves-nut, 163
  preserves-wine, 163
Sausage:
  basic cooking, 106
  bigos, 108
  chorizos, 107
  Italian, 106
  with pasta, 107
  pepperoni, 107
  Polish, and beans, 107
  Polish, ham and noodles, 104
  Polish, and sauerkraut in beer,
    107
Sauerkraut:
  and franks, 100
  and Polish sausage, 107
Sauteeing, 46
Sea Food:

clam chowder, 122
crab cakes, 121
creamed shrimp, 118
Egg Foo Yung, 115
Jambalaya, 119
Lo Mein, 86
she-crab soup, 121
shrimp creole, 122
shrimp and egg, 177
Searing, 46
Separating eggs, 44-45
Sharpener, knife, 11
Shopping:
    amount to buy, 22-23
    list, 21
    menu planning, 21-22
    for one, 57-59
    in rural areas, 18-19
    See also Food
Sifting flour, 44
Simmering, 31-35
    definitions of, 45-46
    with eggs, 127
    pad, 16, 33
Solo-cooking. See one-person
    cooking
Soup:
    cheese, 142
    clam chowder, 122
    cream, 143
    egg drop, 142
    gazpacho, 143
    lentil, 140
    lima bean, 139
    minestrone, 144
    mung bean, 140
    onion, 143
    Polish beet (barszcz), 144
    potato, 140
    potato and cheese, 141
    she-crab, 121
    soy chili, 140
    split pea, 139
    substitute potato, 141
    tuna chowder, 144
    vegetable, 142
Soy (bean), 64-65, 79

chili, 140
    and lamb meatballs, 90
    "meat" balls, 146
    stuffed green peppers, 146
    tacos, 146
Spaghetti. See Pasta
Spam. See Ham
Spices:
    with canned meals, 58
    definition of, 46-47
    with eggs, 127
    kinds to bring, 13
    list of, 188-89
    packing of, 15-16
    storing of, 13, 14, 47, 189
Spinach salad, 155-56
Sprouting, 64, 72-73
Squash and ham, 176
Staples, check list of, 181-82
Steaming, 11
Stock, soup, 73
Stove(s):
    advantages of (vs. fires), 24-25
    built-in features, 29-30
    cold weather use, 29-30
    efficiency of, 27, 31
    fuel capacity of, 28-29
    maintenance, 30, 35
    operation of, 39
    packing of, 14
    personal preference in, 34-35
    safety valve, 33
    selection of, 5-6
    small vs. large, 29, 45
    stability of, 28
    weights of, 28
    windscreen, 30
    See also Fuel; specific stoves:
    Optimus; Phoebus, etc.
Svea 123 stove, 27, 28, 29, 30-31
                    T
Tenderizing meat:
    chemical, 62
    through long cooking, 63, 79
    marinades, 62, 161
    through pounding, 62
Testing for done-ness, 46, 79

Timing, 45-46
Tomato:
    -peanut butter sauce, 160
    salad, 156
Trangia alcohol stove, 26

U

Unleaded gasoline. *See* Fuel

V

Veal:
    kabob, 89
    kidney stew, 89
    kidneys, 89
    Marengo, 88
    stew, 88
Vegetable(s):
    basic cooking, 148-49
    boiling, 149
    garnishes for, 149
    sauteeing, 149
    soup, 142
    steaming, 149
    *See also individual vegetables:*
    Cabbage; Potato, *etc.*
Vegetarian cooking. *See* Natural
    foods

W

Water:
    container, 12
    sources of, 37, 40
Weights and measures, 190
Whipping, 44
White gas. *See* Fuel
Windscreen, stove, 30

Z

Zucchini delight, 150